Date Due

Mar 28'39			
Apr 12'39			
Apr 18 39			
May 1 '39			

SOME CATHOLIC NOVELISTS

SOME CATHOLIC NOVELISTS

THEIR ART AND OUTLOOK

BY

PATRICK BRAYBROOKE, F.R.S.L.

AUTHOR OF

"THE WISDOM OF G. K. CHESTERTON," "NOVELISTS, WE ARE SEVEN,"
"A CHILD'S CHARLES DICKENS," ETC.

LONDON

BURNS OATES & WASHBOURNE LTD.

First printed in 1931

MADE AND PRINTED IN GREAT BRITAIN

TO

AUNT JESSIE

I DEDICATE this book to you for many reasons. It is your volume because of a drive on the " box-seat " hundreds of years ago in Berkshire. It comes to offer itself for your acceptance because of a sweet mountain view from a Rectory window in Old Ireland. I even ask you to take this book because of an early morning stroll on the English and " wrong side " of the sea that rolls away to Ireland. But principally I wish you to have these Essays in remembrance of walks and talks when we dwelt (I inside—you without the walls) in the Abbey of Mount Melleray. For it was there that we learnt, never to forget, that the silence of the Monks was none other than an echo of the Still Small Voice. And we know that in spite of the noise of a world rushing it knows not where, it knows not why, this Still Small Voice still sounds its everlasting challenge that Man, however much he may try, cannot live by bread alone.

ACKNOWLEDGEMENT

My thanks are due to Mr. Cecil Palmer for kindly allowing me to use some material from my volume, " The Wisdom of G. K. Chesterton," published by him.

AUTHOR'S NOTE

IT has often been said that Catholics, no matter what they happen to be writing, bring in (a more favourite phrase is " drag in ") Catholicism. Fortunately this funny little querulous attack hits the right nail a tiny bump on the head. For a Catholic can no more help bringing Catholicism, either stated or implied, into his writings than a historian, writing a history of the world, can help a direct or indirect reference to Rome.

This volume of Essays aims at being chiefly a book of Literary Criticism and Appreciation. At the same time I have not forgotten that Catholics and others who may happen to read it may expect to find some reference to the religious messages that can be discerned in the writings of these Catholic Novelists. I have, therefore, where possible, written something of this aspect of their work.

If we study a Catholic Novelist so that we learn of both his literary art and his religious outlook, we are, I believe, well on the way to knowing a good deal about both the inner and the outer man.

These seven Catholic Novelists lead in the curious and romantic world of fiction. Certain aspects of Catholicism, as I have tried to show, speak from out their books. A discussion of their religious and literary genius combined may perhaps be of some profit to those who wish to know how a Catholic Novelist of the first rank views both his own art and that more difficult art which we call Life.

PATRICK BRAYBROOKE, F.R.S.L.

13 Argyle Square,
     London, W.C. 1.
          Christmas, 1930.

CONTENTS

LIST OF ILLUSTRATIONS

XV

Photograph by Elliott and Fry

GILBERT KEITH CHESTERTON

ESSAY NUMBER ONE

THE PECULIAR NOVELS OF
G. K. CHESTERTON

B

THE PECULIAR NOVELS OF G. K. CHESTERTON

WHEN we come to think about it, there are an extraordinary number of things that Chesterton can do. He can write an essay that ought to be called an essay but is better than most existing essays. He can create a criticism which has the unusual combination of creation and truth. In his study of Charles Dickens, Chesterton created a new critical Dickens. He held a post-mortem on the great Victorian novelist but, and this is important, he gave to the world what I believe to be a true picture of Charles Dickens. He can write a study of Stevenson which is really a study of Stevenson studying himself. He can pour forth week after week, both in the Catholic and secular press, articles which leave his enemies gasping impotently and his friends gasping with delighted amazement. He has constructed the best poem on King Alfred and, incidentally, has given us one of the best contemporary ballads. But Chesterton has never yet written an ordinary novel. I do not think he ever will. For it is only when you begin to know the soul of Chesterton that you realise his surprises

3

are almost non-surprises in that they are distinctly logical.

The majority of novels that are written to-day are not novel. The English mind, in spite of its distinct Protestantism which is of course merely the love for something new, is scared stiff by novelty. There are two classes of people who can dare to give to the literary world something that is new: the one consists of men of genius; the other is composed of fearless heroes. Chesterton delightfully combines both these attributes. He is a hero in the literary sense, which means that he is not afraid of new forms any more than Browning was, and he is also a man of a peculiar and original talent which, I believe, can be called with full truth genius.

When Chesterton, now too many years ago, published his first novel, we who are old enough to remember it, recall the delighted comments of the press. For the moment the professional critics awoke from that after-dinner nap which lasts from Monday to Saturday and is broken on Sunday by a little light reading just for its own sake. "Here," they said, in a chorus of charming croakings, "is something new. We have to admit that after all the avenues of fiction have not been thoroughly explored. Dickens and Thackeray did not set the

4

pattern for all time. Chesterton has done the unexpected—he has given us a new novel and also a novel that is new."

"The Napoleon of Notting Hill" was undoubtedly a daring experiment and it was an experiment that came off. In giving to the public "The Napoleon of Notting Hill," Chesterton obviously assumed that the public would be able to discriminate between a novel that was pure nonsense and a novel in which the nonsense was purely the background of a distinct and untrammelled philosophy. The essence of this now famous novel is, of course, simply a story of the attempted imposition of romance round the drab quarter of Notting Hill. Chesterton was even optimistic enough to suppose that a poet would be interested in romance outside his own poetry. Most poets are dull men, as mankind has a habit of expecting reaction to follow ecstasy. The saints seem to be the sole exception to this rule.

It is as well to give some care to the background of "The Napoleon of Notting Hill," for this novel does express pretty firmly the fundamental position of Chesterton, that in some ways if we are to get romance we must turn things upside down, inside out or drive poor Aladdin to shout rather hopelessly

5

in the streets " Old lamps for new ones." The desire of a novelist or a philosopher to get back, whether in years or culture, to a former state may be due either to a disappointment with present conditions, or a fixed idea (not in an insane sense in any way) that we necessarily as we grow older, whether personally or in history, proceed further and further away from romance. I think it is necessary to observe here that for Chesterton romance is a very flashing and firework affair : it would turn omnibuses into red, white and blue chariots ; it would make conductors of omnibuses conductors of monarchical states ; it would lead an army of crusaders to Clapham Junction and the army would be the army of salvation (really the culture of the Catholic Church) and never by any chance the Salvation Army.

Thus in " The Napoleon of Notting Hill " we have Adam Wayne embodying a big part of the standpoint of Chesterton. Notting Hill is drab because its streets are dingy and grey : it is drab because its inhabitants do not get very far away from Notting Hill in the era in which they happen to live : it is dull because the sound of martial music is seldom heard ; Notting Hill cannot find its soul because it is hidden by the pall of smoke that seldom lifts from the crowded and rather cheap districts of London.

Now I do not wish to be misunderstood if I say that Chesterton sought in his own brain for something to give romance to Notting Hill and brought forth that which was easiest to explore. Notting Hill could be changed inwardly and then by this change be changed outwardly, or it could be changed outwardly and thereby changed inwardly. Chesterton sought the latter. Notting Hill must be changed outwardly. Men's hearts should be reached through their eyes. It was, I say, the easiest way.

Notting Hill should change its heart by changing its face from the early twentieth century to the face of medievalism. The romantic poet, Adam Wayne, would restore medieval grandeur to Notting Hill: he would give a medieval atmosphere to Surbiton, Wimbledon and Clapham. The process of changing the point of view of the inhabitants of Notting Hill by an external imposition is precisely the opposite method to that employed either by Mr. Bernard Shaw or Mr. H. G. Wells. Mr. Shaw would undoubtedly change Notting Hill by compulsory attendance of its inhabitants at lectures on sociology given by members of the Fabian Society: Mr. Wells would impose upon the inhabitants a Utopia which would prove to be a remedy not for Notting Hill but for a district that had been Notting Hill.

As a pure novel " The Napoleon of Notting Hill "
fails. The story is all the time a laughing and serious
philosophy. Sometimes we feel we are in the midst
of a delicate political satire : sometimes we cry out
with bewilderment that this is not " Alice through
the Looking Glass " but Notting Hill through the
Chesterton glass. Sometimes we murmur that this
is a prose poem : at others that it is the psychological
reaction of a number of people who have escaped
from a lunatic asylum. And then quite suddenly
we realise that we are reading a novel.

In spite of the exuberance of the story, the dashing
clash of battle, the sudden and bewildering changes
in fortune, the background of glamour and romance,
" The Napoleon of Notting Hill " is a message that
is sad. It is the message that the world, apart from
the Church, cannot get away from its immediate
epoch. We can no more get Notting Hill back to
the Middle Ages than we can give La Haye Sainte
back to Napoleon. If we are to get Notting Hill
back to the Middle Ages it will be by means of the
little Catholic churches that group together and stem
the paganism of that deplorable desert.

Chesterton, in spite of his laughter in " The
Napoleon of Notting Hill," began his fiction with
rather shadowy tears. The reactions of the Notting

Hill shopkeepers to the poet's suggestion that it might be a good thing to restore romance to Notting Hill, are met with the picturesque and perfectly true affirmations that "romance is all very well but it is probably commercially unsound." This attitude is brought out extraordinarily vividly when Adam Wayne interviews the Notting Hill barber and tries to point out to him that he might substitute for cutting chins with a razor the cutting off of heads with a sword. But the dear little barber, in his little saloon at the back of the tobacco and sweets shop, prefers his certain fourpence a shave to the possibility of being Lord Provost of Notting Hill or Lord High Almoner of Bayswater.

" ' Shaving, sir ? ' inquired that artist from inside his shop.

' War ! ' replied Wayne, standing on the threshold.

' I beg your pardon,' said the other sharply.

' War ! ' said Wayne warmly. ' But not for anything inconsistent with the beautiful and the civilised arts. War for beauty. War for society. War for peace. A great chance is offered you of repelling that slander which, in defiance of the lives of so many artists, attributes poltroonery to

9

those who beautify and polish the surface of our lives. Why should not hairdressers be heroes ? Why should not——'

'Now, you get out,' said the barber irascibly. 'We don't want any of your sort here. You get out.'

And he came forward with the desperate annoyance of a mild person when enraged.

Adam Wayne laid his hand for a moment on the sword, then dropped it.

'Notting Hill,' he said, 'will need her bolder sons'; and he turned gloomily to the toy-shop."

Here Chesterton seems to bring out that clash which nearly always occurs when the man of imagination meets the man who is not by any means unimaginative but, probably rightly, afraid of the unpractical paths that imagination so often lead along. The barber is not a dullard : he is a man who, having a wife and family, is, *ipso facto*, obliged to follow the line of least resistance. Adam Wayne, living on bread and sonnets, can afford the risk of a change of condition more easily. Should the inhabitants of Notting Hill resort to medievalism and armour, the barber might easily find the necessity of buying a new set of operating tools, but the poet would still find that none would read his sonnets. " The Napoleon of Notting Hill " was an excellent type of novel for a new and untried novelist. It taught him whether he could succeed by a line peculiar and original. In the case of Chesterton " The Napoleon of Notting Hill " was an admirable foundation for his later work. It led the public to *expect* Chesterton to write peculiar novels. The peculiar novel cannot hope for the tremendous response that awaits the novel more in line with the tradition of fiction which is not by any means a fiction but a solid truth. Thus, Chesterton as a novelist has always appealed to those who are afraid of the ever-widening of art. Chesterton has never been the Einstein of fiction. Relativity does not apply to his work as a novelist. " The Napoleon of Notting Hill " was the clearest possible indication of this. The imaginary battles that took place at Notting Hill are, I think, but an echo of the real battles that take place in Chesterton's own mind, those battles which are the counterpart of a mind that can always see that it is impossible to understand the donkey's head unless there is knowledge of his tail as well.

From the purely technical standpoint, " The Napoleon of Notting Hill " was for a young writer no inconsiderable achievement. It was obviously far from easy to describe with any degree of reality the battles in Bayswater and Notting Hill. We feel we are the witnesses of a real battle and not a mere kind of hotch-potch battle of cranks. Chesterton even understands military strategy.

The characters in this novel are drawn with a care that does not always distinguish work that is pure fantasy. The king, the poet, the minor characters, stand out from a background which might easily envelop them in obscurity. They are ridiculous, but they are not absurd. The man who stands on his head simply does so to get a different view of the world in much the same way as a man will get a completely different view of religion by studying the conclusions of the irreligious. At the conclusion of " The Napoleon of Notting Hill " we are admitted into the heart of an idealist who will go out to find strange things in the world. He will go out, we feel, perchance enthusiastic. He will perhaps grow tired. He will perchance declare the heavens to be obscured by thick clouds. But at present the sun shines : the birds sing as they must have sung to St Francis, and the world is in the full flush of the disappearing dawn.

Auberon and Adam Wayne go out into the

universe to search for wild roses as the two young men so charmingly written of in " Intentions " by Oscar Wilde went out while the silver dawn fed London out of a goblet of silver. Let us leave them starting on their pilgrimage, happy for, as they say, " laughter and love are everywhere." So shall the necessity of poetry and culture be a necessity to the world. That is perhaps one small part of the Catholic message of Chesterton.

*　　　*　　　*　　　*　　　*

With his next novel Chesterton took a decided step further. His canvas became broader, his picture more intricate, his art more " intelligent." In " The Napoleon of Notting Hill " Chesterton had been really a satirist. In " The Man who was Thursday " he becomes almost a preacher. He has left behind a philosophy of romance and has created something that may be called a philosophy of reality. Perhaps in some small way Chesterton felt—I think almost unconsciously—that he had neglected in " The Napoleon of Notting Hill " the possibilities of romance that underlay the outward reality. Why do I suggest that there is romance in the reality of " The Man who was Thursday ? " Because— and this is a fundamental of Chesterton—things are seldom if ever what they seem. Which position may, of course, drive us to ecstasy or drive us to suicide.

As a novel "The Man who was Thursday" is both sane and insane. It is sane in the sense that the apparently insane is quite sane and it is insane in as much as we consider anything unusual to be insane. The situation in this really remarkable novel is certainly grotesque, and though Chesterton takes us into a kind of Lewis Carroll atmosphere he is by no means the Mad Hatter. There is method in his madness, and I know of no better sanity than the madness of Chesterton.

The story in the novel can be dismissed in a few words. We are introduced to a pleasant little mix-up in which a number of anarchists are simply policemen in disguise. We are more accustomed to the reverse position. The anarchists are in charge of a rather peculiar President with the quite appropriate name of Sunday. In creating Sunday, Chesterton boldly allied himself with the artists who have not been afraid of a figure who might conceivably engulf their whole canvas. Sunday might quite conceivably be too much for Chesterton. Chesterton equally easily might prove too much for Sunday. As a matter of fact, the two collaborate excellently.

This novel is, of course, a discussion on anarchy,

that ridiculous creed which thinks that by killing a king it will kill the monarchy. As a matter of mere historical interest, the monarchy has nearly always been killed by the kings. Chesterton attacks anarchy in the same way that Dickens attacked Mr. Bumble. He laughs at it. It is rather a foolish little game of chess : it is using a repeating revolver to kill a repeating decimal : it is an argument in a circle : it might almost be called a journey round the Inner Circle.

While one part of " The Man who was Thursday " concerns the contention that things are not what they seem, another vital part of the novel demands with almost vulgar insistence, with a complete disregard of our feelings, that we never know anybody. This is, of course, a contention that is not quite true, unless there is added the explanation that we never know anybody because we never know ourselves.

Syme is the type of man that Chesterton detests. He is the type of man who, mistaking his back-garden for the whole world, claims all knowledge, quite forgetting that he has not even the minutest knowledge of a blade of grass. With a tremendous burst of enthusiasm—that burst of enthusiasm which always heralds a tremendous lie—Syme declares, " I see everything," and yet perhaps the assertion is not so pernicious as that of the shouting, ranting orator who howls at his astonished listeners that "it is all nonsense, all nonsense," quite forgetting that the only nonsense is that which appears to him to be sense.

It is almost surprising sometimes to discover in Chesterton's fiction the tremendously deep truths that lie behind a sentence that in its context may occur in a passage almost flippant. Thus, when one of the policemen holds forth as probably no policeman in fact would hold forth, Chesterton allows him to say almost in passing this very superb piece of rational philosophy : "We say," says the policeman, "that the most dangerous criminal now is the entirely lawless modern philosopher." He is, obviously, the most dangerous of intellectual experimenters for his astounding and almost incredible fallacies are supported by a kind of scholarship which is palatable to the masses who cannot discover that the use of philosophical terms by no means postulates the philosopher. The modern lawless philosopher, as Chesterton would insist, I am certain, uses all his dialectics to destroy the Church, only to find that what Chesterton calls " the five deaths of the faith " will in future have to be called the six deaths of the faith. For what has your modern lawless philosopher done ? He has inflicted a sixth death on the Church : he has killed a few people's bodies : he has wounded a few souls : and after a short and falsely triumphant progress he finds that to lose the soul he so denies would be a fate out of all proportion to that which he deserves.

In an essay like this in which one attempts on a very small canvas to give a picture that has almost endless possibilities, it is obviously necessary to attempt to show something of the versatility of the subject one hopes to paint. In the preceding paragraph I gave a small example of Chesterton using fiction for the discussion of a serious philosophy. We should have an extremely inadequate portrait of Chesterton as a novelist if we did not find in the picture some example of his whimsical and delicious humour. There is a delightful piece of Chesterton humour when Syme seeks a quarrel with the Marquis de Saint Eustache. The whole style is most charming. Almost for the moment we feel that the passage before us has not been written by a twentieth-century writer but by a nineteenth-century writer of curious genius and tragedy—Oscar Wilde. I have been unable to discover in Chesterton's writings any more marked passage bearing Wilde influence than this one which I give here.

The background is of course quite simple. Syme has just complained that the Marquis, who really wants to be left alone to eat caviare and drink light sparkling wine, has insulted him. A few lines will, I think, indicate the humour of Chesterton quite convincingly :

"' This man has insulted me !' said Syme, with gestures of explanation.

' Insulted you ? ' cried the gentleman with the red rosette, ' When ? '

' Oh, just now,' said Syme recklessly. ' He insulted my mother.'

' Insulted your mother !' exclaimed the gentleman incredulously.

' Well, anyhow,' said Syme, conceding a point, ' my aunt.'

' But how can the Marquis have insulted your aunt just now ? ' said the second gentleman with some legitimate wonder. ' He has been sitting here all the time.'

' Ah, it was what he said !' said Syme darkly.

' I said nothing at all,' said the Marquis, ' except something about the band. I only said that I liked Wagner played well.'

'It was an allusion to my family,' said Syme firmly. 'My aunt played Wagner badly. It was a painful subject. We are always being insulted about it.'"

Suppose without reading too much into "The Man who was Thursday" we asked the question "Is there a Catholic message in this early fiction of Chesterton?" I think that without reading too much into an odd sentence it may be said that Chesterton's real Catholic outlook, which has always been there, whether definitely expressed or only suggested, is absolutely to be found when he writes this profound and unalterable truth:

"Yet this one old Christian lantern you shall not destroy——"

and I almost wish that Chesterton had added: "Lo, I am with you always, even unto the end of the world."

One more amazing passage must be given, when the magnificently conceived character Sunday explains or defines the incredible force or personality that he is. For Sunday is that indefinable something that men and women seek, that indefinable something that grows larger and larger as the day of death grows nearer and nearer, that indefinable something which drives men into the contemplative walk with God, that indefinable something that brought forth from Pilate the cry of all humanity, " What is truth ? " Syme asks Sunday what he is, and the answer is that answer which was said in more simple language in answer to the questionings of the Jews, " Before Abraham was, I am."

" ' And you,' said Syme, leaning forward, ' what are you ? '

' I ? What am I ? ' roared the President, and he rose slowly to an incredible height, like some enormous wave about to arch above them and break. ' You want to know what I am, do you ? Bull, you are a man of science. Grub in the roots of those trees and find out the truth about them. Syme you are a poet. Stare at those morning clouds. But I tell you this, that you will have found out the truth of the last tree and the topmost cloud before the truth about me. You will understand the sea, and I shall be still a riddle ; you shall know what the stars are, and not know what I am. Since the beginning of the world all men have hunted me like a wolf—kings and sages, and poets and law-givers, all the churches and all the philosophies. But I have never been caught yet, and the skies will fall in the time I turn to bay. I have given them a good run for their money, and I will now.' "

" The Man who was Thursday " is an extravaganza, a philosophy, a humorous novel, a book of religion, and, as Chesterton describes it, a nightmare, except that unlike most nightmares, it is, in spite of its apparent madness, completely sane. I have only one hostile criticism to the book, and it is that the title is extraordinarily bad. The proper title should be " The Man who was Chesterton."

*　　*　　*　　*　　*

In a later novel, " Manalive," Chesterton gives us a really psychological novel. He is the student of human conduct : he is concerned with that most difficult of all problems, the problem of motive. He advances a theory which has already been indicated in some small measure in " The Napoleon of Notting Hill " and in " The Man who was Thursday," that a good way—perhaps the only way —to understand reality is to do in a more exaggerated fashion what Plato did—not consider the world of ideas to be the real one but to consider that in many respects reality (the goal of all philosophy), whether false or true, is the world of ideas upside down.

The story that lies behind " Manalive " is an example of that ingenuous type of tale in which the sting is in the tail of each situation. Innocent Smith is a type that Chesterton is really fond of. He is in a way a " criminal " with a mission. He sets out to find whether people do not mean what they say. He is no more disappointed in his search than we are. The background of the story is strangely reminiscent of Jerome's most famous work, " The Passing of the Third Floor Back," only in this case it is really the passing of the first floor front. Innocent Smith creates a stir in a boarding house because boarding houses are not used to innocent people, and he creates a bigger stir by the fact that he is a horrid criminal. But if he is a criminal, he is a criminal not because he wants to commit crime but because he is forced to show the kindness of crime. For the moment let us glance at a certain Chesterton discussion which is of course the *raison d'être* of " Manalive."

Chesterton writes thus concerning the fact that we are singularly without perception in matters of crime and crime prevention. We treat criminals as criminals when they should be treated as patients : we treat lunatics as lunatics when a change of scene would mean a change of outlook.

We call in the State instead of calling in the family doctor.

" It is true that there's too much official and indirect power. Often and often the thing a whole nation can't settle is just the thing a family could settle. Scores of young criminals have been fined and sent to jail when they ought to have been thrashed and sent to bed. Scores of men, I am sure, have had a lifetime at Hanwell when they only wanted a week at Brighton."

Though Innocent Smith is accused of several criminal charges it will be quite sufficient for us to examine one of them, always remembering that Chesterton is a most imposing figure on the only judicial bench he will ever occupy—the bench made for judicial novelists. We will take the most serious crime of all with which Innocent Smith is charged, that of murder. When Innocent Smith is asked why he carries about with him an enormous revolver, his reply gives us the clue to the nature of his deplorable crime. Smith answers the question about his revolver with a paradox which is paradoxical enough to be untrue. He replies that his revolver is an instrument for dealing out life. That is, of course, merely Chesterton shooting with a revolver and holding it the wrong end.

Smith has been accused of attempting to shoot at a college professor, the type of person who is usually only shot at by metaphysicians. Professor Eames is a thorough-going philosopher of the pessimist school. He demands, like Schopenhauer (who was always careful that his theories did not apply to himself), that the greatest happiness man can expect is rapid extinction. Dr. Eames is expounding his pessimistic theory to Innocent Smith. The professor, living according to rule, expects that his listener will comment on his pessimistic deductions by the usual " Is that so, Sir ? I suppose, Sir, such a school of thought might be called either heroic or cowardly according to one's predilections." Instead of which, Professor Eames is for once really taken seriously. Or perhaps it is more true to say that he is taken literally. There is perhaps no greater surprise that we can experience than being taken seriously. Innocent Smith really does believe that Professor Eames wishes to die, whereas, as a matter of fact, what he is really saying is, " The pain of life is so inevitable that it is really absurd to embark upon the voluntary pain connected with the will to live." In other words, the Professor would say quite cheerily, " Let us eat, drink and be merry, for to-day we die, only let us be sure that the conclusion is not reached until to-morrow."

The delightful and whimsical picture that Chesterton gives us of Smith's crime is in this manner :

" ' To anyone who thinks,' proceeded Eames, ' the pleasures of life, trivial and soon tasteless, are bribes to bring us into a torture chamber. We all see that for any thinking man mere extinction is the . . . What are you doing ? . . . Are you mad ? . . . Put that thing down.'

Dr. Eames had turned his tired but still talkative head over his shoulder, and had found himself looking into a small round black hole, rimmed by a six-sided circlet of steel, with a sort of spike standing up on the top. It fixed him like an iron eye. Through those eternal instants during which the reason is stunned he did not even know what it was. Then he saw behind it the chambered barrel and cocked hammer of a revolver, and behind that the flushed and rather heavy face of Smith, apparently quite unchanged, or even more mild than before.

'I'll help you out of your hole, old man,' said Smith, with rough tenderness. 'I'll put the puppy out of his pain.'

Emerson Eames retreated towards the window. 'Do you mean to kill me?' he cried.

'It's not a thing I'd do for everyone,' said Smith with emotion; 'but you and I seem to have got so intimate to-night, somehow. I know all your troubles now, and the only cure, old chap.'

'Put that thing down,' shouted the Warden.

'It'll soon be over, you know,' said Smith with the air of a sympathetic dentist. And as the Warden made a run for the window and balcony, his benefactor followed him with a firm step and a compassionate expression.''

It is then obvious that the Chesterton lesson behind this is twofold. Firstly, that the will to die is not the genuine reaction of a man of sanity, and secondly that the real menace to man's well-being is not brought about by men like Innocent Smith but by theoretical humbugs who rant their pernicious theories safe in the knowledge that none will take them quite seriously.

And there is a third and deeper meaning behind this Chesterton ingenious fooling. It is that pessimism is not only a lie but a blasphemy, an insult to the glory of the stars, a gibe at the heat of the sun, a sneer at the birds as they float across the blue sky, gently gliding from cloud to cloud, a base ingratitude to the Being who staggered up the long hill out of Jerusalem, that we might build the New Jerusalem which should be called by all men The City of God. For, shouts Chesterton, rather than be pessimistic you shall be optimistic—" you shall thank heaven for churches and chapels and villas and vulgar people and puddles and pots and pans and sticks and rags and bones and spotted blinds."

In " Manalive " Chesterton almost formulates a new philosophy. It is the philosophy of life looked at upside down : it is not quite a new philosophy because it is the old Catholic philosophy, which from the point of view of the world always seems too good to be true, when, as a matter of fact, it is too good to be untrue. Chesterton could not formulate a new philosophy for there is no new philosophy. He gives us in " Manalive " a little more from the real store of Revelation.

We may then proceed to discover Chesterton jumping down, as it were, from the heights of philosophy to the lower heights of sociology on which he stands in his remarkable novel " The Flying Inn." In this book Chesterton is concerned with a direct attack on the problem of prohibition. A terrible fate has overtaken England and this is but one result :

> " The wicked old women who feel well bred
> Have turned to a tea shop the Saracen's Head."

The main theme of " The Flying Inn " is the fight of the last innkeeper for his inn. This fight represents Chesterton's fight against the policy which demands that a thing which can be bad is of necessity bad intrinsically. It is no valid argument against drink that men get drunk, is his position. For I do not think that it is exaggerating Chesterton's outlook to say that prohibition might almost be termed a subtle blasphemy. For prohibition implies that God's good gift is a bad one. He seems to say that what we require in the matter of drink, as in everything else, is temperance rather than abstinence.

Apart from the excellence of the argument in " The Flying Inn," this novel is most valuable, showing us as it does some of the most charming and whimsical of Chesterton's verses. The Irish captain who recites so much poetry to the innkeeper is a pleasing character. One of the most excellent poems which he recites is that one which is a lesson in the etiquette to which we should have to conform were we so honoured as to have St George as a visitor to tea. The poem, written with that music which is a part of Chesterton at his best as a poet, may perhaps almost be called an ode to hospitality. It represents the essence of "The Flying Inn." It demands that English hospitality is a poor thing if the only attributes are tea and coffee. For, says Chesterton, you would not dare to give a man beans unless you gave him bacon, and you simply cannot treat him to cakes unless you treat him to ale. The poem in the light sense carries with it the spirit of Dickens. If we seek for a deeper meaning, it may well be that we must be quite certain that none of our sociological reforms should ignore the fact that God once said, "Thou hast kept the good wine until now."

> " Saint George he was for England,
> And before he killed the dragon
> He drank a pint of English ale
> Out of an English flagon.
> For though he fast right readily
> In hair shirt or in mail,
> It isn't safe to give him cakes
> Unless you give him ale.

" Saint George he was for England,
And right gallantly set free
The lady left for dragon's meat
And tied up to a tree ;
But since he stood for England
And knew what England means,
Unless you give him bacon
You mustn't give him beans.

" Saint George he is for England,
And shall wear the shield he wore
When we go out in armour
With the battle cross before.
And though he is jolly company
And very pleased to dine,
It isn't safe to give him nuts
Unless you give him wine."

" The Flying Inn " is again the expression of a Chestertonian opposition to a pessimism which expresses itself in the suggestion that a possible poison is of necessity a poison. It denies that grapes can only be eaten : it might even demand that prohibition was only sour grapes. Yet again Chesterton thunders from the highest heavens : " Thou fool, dost thou not see that all the things of God are good ? Who makes them bad ? Dost thou not see that the drunkard is not a reproach to the inn-keepers but a reproach to the inmost soul of man ?

Dost thou not see that the prohibitionist is pointing the coward's way out ? Dost thou not see that the temperate drinker gives good account of his stewardship of life ? "

I can but merely mention two other novels that Chesterton has given us. There is " The Ball and the Cross," a splendid argument between an atheist and a believer. And there is " The Return of Don Quixote," which is again a novel something on the lines of " The Napoleon of Notting Hill."

There is one challenging question in " The Return of Don Quixote " that Chesterton hurls at his modern readers :

"St Francis was a popular leader. If you saw a leper walking across this lawn, would you rush at him and embrace him ? "

There is no need to ask what a Catholic would reply.

*   *   *   *   *

As a novelist Chesterton has a valuable and direct message for those who are members of the Catholic Church. And the message is this : You cannot get away from optimism except by blindness. You cannot escape the mercy of God either in the depths of the ocean or on the heights of the mountains.

It is the blind who really see God : it is the deaf who hear his voice : it is the dumb who chant his praises.

The novels of Chesterton are really new. He has not started any new school in novel writing for the very good reason that none of the pupils could follow the master. His fiction is eccentric but it does not pose. He gives it its head, but it does not run away with him. The Chesterton fiction style is the Chesterton fiction style, and there is little more to be said. It jumps from paradox to paradox and each paradox is a step in the ladder that leads to truth.

No just criticism can be levelled against Chesterton that his characters do not reveal themselves sufficiently. They are lovable, though they wear tremendous hats. They are delightful, though they stand on their heads in our back garden. They are more than charming because so many of them prefer hansom cabs to motor-cars. Possibly apart from the main Catholic message that I have suggested above as to be found in Chesterton's fiction, there are two fundamental positions underlying his philosophy. The one is that the unexpected is not necessarily good : the other is that romance lies in our own room, in our own house, and even in the mirror.

And if we would look for the greatest of all lessons, it can be found at the back of Chesterton's novels.

It is this. We have to follow a long road that winds backwards to sanity, a long road that has cut its way through the mountains of heresy and misunderstanding, a long road that leads back to a little village on the first Christmas night, to which all the wise men from the East and the West and the North and the South must eventually go.

Camera Portrait by E. O. Hoppé

HILAIRE BELLOC

ESSAY NUMBER TWO

HILAIRE BELLOC AS A NOVELIST

HILAIRE BELLOC AS A NOVELIST

THERE is an interesting and possibly not unpractical psychological value in the question which asks why a writer of fame in several walks in literature should embark upon periodic excursions into fiction. There is the vulgar and popular answer given by the worldly cynic, who is of all men the most ignorant, that the writing of fiction is a good commercial proposition. This answer is in itself more often than not a fiction. Should the answer be true, we are in danger of stating that all conversion from one form of literature to another has no higher motive than money. But there is another—and in my opinion a deeper—reason why a critic may become a novelist or a novelist (which is much more rare) become a critic. The mind of the man of letters is in danger always of becoming narrowed into a groove. Force of circumstances quite often drives a writer along a certain path. The more successful he is the more often will he find himself unable to launch out. Therefore periodic excursions into fiction probably more truly indicate fear of insularity than anything else. It may be, of course, the surrender to a sudden inspiration, but more often than not it is, I think, a wish to be versatile and a refusal to be the expected.

It would be bordering upon exaggeration to describe Belloc as a novelist and mean the same thing as when we say that Bennett is a novelist or Walpole is a writer of fiction. Bennett and Walpole are novelists who periodically make excursions into the more serious side of literature : Belloc is a serious writer who makes periodic excursions into the realms of fiction. That they are accompanied by extraordinary success does not alter the fact that they are excursions even in the sense that they are almost holidays. And I am not sure that the last word in the preceding sentence does not explain rather well Belloc's psychological reaction to the call of fiction. For his novels are a holiday : they depart a very long way (not in quality) from Belloc telling us of the French Revolution, Belloc letting us hear the thud of the guillotine, as with true democracy it decapitates first the royal house of France and then Robespierre, the Dictator of the Republic that was to be. It is a holiday from Belloc telling us once again of what Europe owes to the Catholic Church and what it has lost by the inroads of a bitter and bigoted Protestantism. Belloc's holiday is again even a long way from " The Four Men " who journey and discuss so delightfully together : it is far from the sweet downs of Sussex and it is not very near " The Bad Child's Book of Beasts."

Recognising that Belloc is on a holiday when he is writing novels we need feel no surprise at receiving from him a mixture of politics, humour and philosophy, mixed up in a highly ingenious and diverting story. There is always in whatever Belloc writes more than meets the eye. There is this kind of attribute in many of our modern novelists, but it is just as well to point out that what does not meet the eye is better not met at all.

Three of Belloc's most charming works of fiction, " The Green Overcoat," " Mr. Petre," and " The Emerald," display most if not all of the qualities that are characteristic of Belloc's novels. " The Green Overcoat " is a very excellent treatise dealing with the horrid but inevitable platitude that small beginnings lead to big events, and also that borrowing without asking may not be so criminal as stealing, but is likely to cause the person involved equal inconvenience. The plot of " The Green Overcoat " is almost absurdly simple in its kernel, but the shell that grows round it is complicated, diverse and even problematic.

If there is one kind of person who brings out

Belloc's kindly satire it is the rather self-satisfied gentle Professor. Professor Higginson is complacent, gentle, a specialist both by profession and thought, and slightly untidy. At the beginning of the story poor Professor Higginson is in a quandary that all his academic learning cannot get him out of without resort to bold, bad, reckless crime. Professor Higginson at the end of the party to which he has been invited finds that, regardless of the fact that he has forgotten his overcoat, the rain falls outside in torrents. The Professor of Psychology, hating rain as a thing of spitting insult, borrows a Green Overcoat intending to return it to his host the first thing in the morning. Belloc launches the Professor in this manner on his career of curious adventure :

" It was all right. He would pretend some mistake, and send it back the *very first thing* next morning ; nay, he would be an honest man, and send it back *at once* by a messenger the moment he found out his mistake on getting to his lodgings. So wealthy an overcoat could only belong to a great man—a man who would stay late, very late. Come, the Green Overcoat would be back again in that house before its owner had elected to move.

He would be no wiser ! There was no harm done, and he could not walk as he was through the rain."

It is worth adding to this little dramatic scene the kind of little ethical precept which Belloc writes. For though we have no understanding whatever of crime or criminals except to think that punishment fits the crime, we do know that it is the plausible and deadly argument which makes a wrong act appear only a little wrong that is the cause of all crimes whether light or serious. Thus Belloc writes with quaint, almost archaic diction, of the way in which the Professor's plausible arguments for borrowing the Green Overcoat were the base of his fall :

" Alas ! These plausible arguments proceeded, had the Professor but known it, from the Enemy of Souls ! *He*, the fallen archangel, foresaw that coming ruin to which his lanky and introspective victim was unhappily blind. Dons are cheap meat for Devils."

Mr. Kirby, a solicitor who is the type of solicitor always keen on improving the occasion, is drawn in vast contrast to Professor Higginson. In between them there is Mr. Brassington, who is best described

41

rather crudely as being full of brass. He is prosperous, commercial, good-natured, dull, full of sayings that were quite clever when first originated. There is a considerable difference, again, between Brassington and Kirby. Brassington, in a parrot-like fashion, ejaculates pious opinions : Kirby invariably adds to them and deduces some general principle from them. It is Belloc telling us all the time that even trivial conversation need not necessarily be trivial in thought. Thus when Mr. Brassington says the tremendous and rather dreadful truth that " Long habit affects men," Mr. Kirby expands this cryptic remark into a tremendous truism which is the fundamental reason why men, unless they be either insane through misfortune or through sceptical thought, cling to life. It is once again Belloc telling us through the medium of a few chance remarks, that our most deep-set fears are caused by an almost unconscious universal emotion spreading itself from one person to another like an infection. And the antidote to the dictum pronounced by Mr. Kirby, *alias* Belloc, is the Catholic Church.

" ' Of course it does,' said Mr. Kirby, with the fullest sympathy. ' That is why so many people are afraid of death. They're afraid of the change of habit.' "

If Belloc is ever aware of the tragedy that lies behind comedy, he is equally fully aware of the comedy, even the humour, possibly the farce, that arises out of tragedy. Poor Professor Higginson mistaken for Mr. Brassington has been incarcerated in a kind of prison for the abominable reason of financial extraction by force. Belloc introduces us to a really ludicrous situation which I do not think could quite be given us by any other fiction writer of to-day. We find the Professor, having made valiant efforts to escape from his prison, flung unwittingly on to the floor. But, being a Professor, he is ever conscious of the necessity of never failing to let any situation acquire for himself new knowledge. Finding that he was unable to escape from the ropes that bound him to his chair, the Professor assuming the rôle of a tortoise, takes the chair with him. Thus we have a glimpse of Belloc providing us with a new beast for a bad child, namely, Professor Higginson crawling round a room with a chair on his back. The mixture of nonsense and enterprise, the portrait of a practical issue forced upon a theorist, the mixture of academic satire and academic admiration for the wish to learn something out of everything, is Belloc in one of his happiest moods :

> " In this native posture he was capable of progression, of progression with the chair burdening his back like the shell of a tortoise, and with his legs dragged numbly after him, but still of progression, for he could put one hand before the other after the fashion of a wounded bear, and so drag the remainder of his person in their wake.
>
> In this fashion, as the light gradually broadened on the filthy and deserted apartment, Professor Higginson began an Odyssey, painful and slow, all over the floor of his prison. He inspected its utmost corners in search of something sharp wherewith to cut the cord, but nothing sharp was to be found."

It seems to be more than difficult for Belloc to keep out of his writing frequent allusions to matters of our national deportment and manners. Now in " The Green Overcoat " Belloc very truly searches out the fact that professors are a cause of rather good-natured amusement. Their idiosyncrasies, their forgetfulness, their pedantry, their airs of superiority—not snobbish superiority but intellectual superiority—are a never-failing source of supply to the humorous papers of which " Punch " cannot claim to be guiltless. The poorer classes— I mean the men and women who really do count their pennies not because they are interested in arithmetic but because they are interested in bread— look upon professors as beings as remote as the mammals who reside in our national museums. Thus, when Belloc remarks that the poor will welcome the wealthy if they look without knowledge of the realities of life, he is simply saying that though a man is a poor man, he is not of necessity a poor sportsman. The poor man is sorry for the duke who except for his father's riches would be too poor to buy bread : he is sorry for the professor who enters a public-house and who could lecture on every chemical contained in beer, but who has no idea how to ask for a pint to drink. And I am afraid that Belloc is only too right when he insists that the poor love to see the rich showing signs of dissipation. In such a condition for once in his life the poor man feels (and is) superior to the rich man, superior not only morally but even physically, knowing that with all his poverty he has a firmer hold of his own soul than the rich man with all his riches. So Belloc writes only too truly of the pleasure the Professor's tattered appearance gives to the night-watchmen who

45

see in him the incarnation of " a bloke who has made a night of it."

" If the mass of our people love a guileless simplicity in their superiors, when it is accompanied by debauch they positively adore it ; and the excellent reception the Professor met with upon his entry was due more than anything else to the conviction of his three inferiors that an elderly man in tattered evening clothes and abominable linen must have spent the night before in getting outrageously drunk."

The main part of " The Green Overcoat " is a subtle attack on all the nonsense and vulgarity which is connected with occultism. There is no need to follow the curious course that gets Professor Higginson into the rôle of a false psychic expert, but we may discover with profit a little of what happens to him when he assumes this undesired and unlooked-for rôle. There is a truly delightful description when Professor Higginson deals with the mass of correspondence that is launched upon him since " The Howl " has declared him to be the man who had proved life after death. Belloc is showing us by some charming satire the gullibility of the public who will accept any experience however vague and unsatisfactory so long as it is unorthodox and sensational. Professor Higginson is really a man of extremely little importance, but his pronouncement that life proceeds after physical dissolution is hailed as great news by those who would be quite cold to the same fact which has been handed down through the centuries by the divine authority of the Church. Though Belloc amuses us, we cannot help feeling amazed and irritated that the mass public is without intelligence, perception or even any sense of the artistic. But here is Belloc showing us dear Professor Higginson overwhelmed with letters—one of those men whose fame is so terrific that it bursts like an enormous star and lasts as long as a firework.

" Professor Higginson had never written to such great men before. He worked really hard, and he composed two masterpieces. Upon the addressing of his first ten envelopes he spent the best part of twenty minutes with books of reference at his side. He wrote courteously and at enormous length to a Great Lady whose coronet stood out upon the paper like a mountain, and whose signature he could yet hardly accept as real, so tremendous a thing did it seem to him that such an one as She should have entered his life.

He wrote in extraordinary French to the great Specialist at Nancy who had written to him in English. He wrote in English to the great Specialist of Leipsic who had written to him in a German he did not understand, but whose signature and European name warranted the nature of the reply. So passed all Saturday's leisure."

Professor Higginson's excursion into psychic fame gives Belloc an excellent opportunity of making a small attack on the Sunday newspapers. His attack is not so much on the matter of the Sunday newspapers as on the ridiculous lack of any critical faculties that they possess. The Sunday press is, with the exception of one or two of the better class papers, completely hypnotised by the last little piece of sensation. Thus, when the Sunday newspapers have on their placards the startling question, " Is there a Heaven ? " we might well suppose that such a question might be asked by a theologian. Instead of which we find that it is merely a rather smart and shallow little sub-editor (who lives admirably at Golders Green on nine guineas a week) doing his job very well journalistically and making poor Professor Higginson for the moment a man of considerable news value. There is, then,

48

Professor Higginson roared at during the peace of a Sunday morning by the Sunday placards which reside so arrogantly outside the shop which sells sweets to men and cigarettes to women. Belloc is enjoying his holiday tremendously : he can even have a dig at the press without covering his digging in the firm earth of a severe and painstaking essay :

> " The Sunday Popular Papers were hot on his trail. Their great flaring placards stood outside the news shops.
> ' Is there a Heaven ? ' in letters a foot long, and underneath, ' Professor Higginson says " Yes," ' almost knocked him down as they stared at him from one hoarding. In the loud bill outside a chapel he saw his name set forth as the ' subject of the discourse ' and before he could snatch away his eyes he had caught the phrase : ' The First Witness.' All were welcome. . . . *He* was the First Witness ! . . . Oh, God ! "

Professor Higginson is a Belloc man of the moment. His moment gives us many ideas of moment. He is the centre of a good-natured yet profound Belloc philosophy. Professor Higginson shows us the futility of attempting to prove spiritual

E

truths by physical manifestations. Professor Higginson also makes us think anew not about crime, but about the embryonic process of thought and action which is potential crime. Professor Higginson had had his short day of fame and let us leave the worthy professor of psychology dawdling about his lecture-room. Let us leave him chastened and humbled by his sudden and unexpected notoriety : let us leave him basking in the genial sun of theory. Let us turn to Mr. Petre arriving at Plymouth from one of those gigantic American liners which do not prove in the very slightest that man can conquer the sea, but prove rather that however much man may build he can no more conquer the sea than he can put out burning mountains with new-fashioned water-works.

* * * * *

" Mr. Petre " demonstrates a rather encouraging truth and a truth that is specially encouraging for the still comparatively few people who are clever enough to write novels. It is the truth that an old story is seldom old in new hands. Loss of identity is a theme as old in English literature as English literature itself. It can lead to two emotional situations. On the one hand broad comedy : on the other narrow and inevitable tragedy. But there is a third contingency, and it is one that will occur more readily to the artist whether he paint with a pen or a brush than to the far more important individual—the bulk of our population—the non-creative but receptive artists. That contingency is the cheerful knowledge that a novelist, if he be a true novelist in the sense that he cannot help telling a story, need not look for necessarily new ideas, for he will know that his own interpretation of his well-worn theme will almost of necessity supply that novelty so essential to a work of fiction.

Loss of identity gives to Belloc the third and exclusive contingency which I have mentioned above. Though in " Mr. Petre " he deals with this time-worn theme, he has given us a really new novel. He has quite obviously admitted to himself that it is a law that the new is not an objective stimulus exclusively, but a subjective urge. Belloc in " Mr. Petre " is still in full enjoyment of his fiction holiday. His work literally sings its way along like a care-free tramp singing over the rise and fall of the Sussex Downs. But, as in all Belloc's work, there are heavy truths which cannot be obscured even by light fiction. The background of the story is ordinary, but it is not ordinary enough to be commonplace with a vague possibility of the intrusion of the banal. Mr. Petre arrives back from America, passes through the customs, declares in front of those terrible people, takes his place in the boat train—the most delightful experience after six or seven days at the mercy of the sea and the cabin stewards—the boat train starts for London and Mr. Petre loses his memory. It is probable that of all situations there can be none more distressing than a loss of memory with a train whirling its victim at sixty miles an hour to the ungenial and deadly complacency of London.

When Mr. Petre loses his memory we find Belloc giving us something of his tremendous powers of description which established themselves so firmly in the describing of the terrible days when men behind shuttered windows listened to the rumble of the tumbrils, sensed the fall of the bloody heads of the guillotine's victims and knew that ere another dawn had come they too might ride in the creaking tumbrils, while from behind other shuttered windows pale men and pale women looked, hoping that they might see and fearing lest they might be seen.

So Belloc writes while the Plymouth boat train hurls itself through the smiling countryside, as though eager to launch its human cargo into the boiling mäelstrom that surrounds Praed Street :

" Then overwhelmingly, in a flash, the truth broke upon him. He had lost all conception of his past : every image of it. He knew where he was. All about him, the landscape, the type of railway carriage—everything was familiar, but of any name or place or action or movement *in connection with himself* prior to that sleep nothing whatsoever remained.

He passed his hand across his forehead, and stared at the empty cushions opposite him, waiting for this very unpleasant mental gap to close up, and for his normal self to return. It did not return. What was worse, he felt a sort of certitude within him that it was gone for ever— that it was no good looking for it. It was as though he had died."

We may skip over Mr. Petre jogging along in the taxi : we may skip over Mr. Petre entering the Hôtel Splendide, one of those huge hotels in which money can buy everything except humanity, and we may find him mistaken for a famous man, discovering himself the guest of Mrs. Cyril, one of those perfect

53

hostesses who never offend anybody as they never by any chance say what they mean. Belloc with an almost sudden startling change, turns from being the sympathetic descriptive artist to being the amused observer of the insincerity that is the sole sincerity of which society is capable. At Mrs. Cyril's luncheon party we have a glimpse of the delightful power Belloc has of depicting the kind of dialogue that takes place while three or four butlers feed the guests who never know what it is to feel hungry. It is difficult to discover a more excellent piece of character creation than when Belloc tells us that Marjorie Kayle can so readily understand Mr. Petre's dislike of press publicity because she was perpetually in the papers. So Belloc lets us into the hearing of the conversation of two ex-Lord Chancellors, whose only difference of life in and out of office is that in office they attended public luncheons, out of office they attended private luncheons :

"' Oh, I can understand that,' sighed Marjorie Kayle, who was perpetually in the papers ; and the two ex-Lord Chancellors agreed. But the kind old Cabinet Minister, putting up his left hand to his ear, only said ' What ? ' and beamed.

54

' Petre,' bellowed Mrs. Cyril into his better ear.
' Petre. The American man. John K. Petre.'

' Oh, the American man,' said the kind old
Cabinet Minister, his face suddenly changing, and
assuming the expression proper to a revelation.
' Not J. K. Petre, the rotor man ? '

' Yes,' roared Mrs. Cyril again. ' The rotor
man, J. K. Petre.'

' I can't conceive,' said the noble poetess,
' what possible good it can do a man to have so
much money.'

' I don't see what possible harm it can do him,'
said Marjorie Kayle with asperity, for she herself,
poor darling, felt strongly on that point ; she
resented the great wealth of the woman who had
just spoken."

There are many attributes which distinguish the
writer who is " in the front rank," a phrase much
more military than literary. Nevertheless the phrase
must stand. The front rank writer is distinguished
by an ease of expression or its opposite, which is not
really difficulty of expression but complicated expression. He is distinguished by an ability to describe
a scene that can be seen. He is distinguished by a
lucidity of argument if he be a serious writer or a

penetration of character if he be a novelist. But there is another attribute which has been in the skin of most of the literary masters. It is a thing which seems so simple that many pass it by. It is not the use of the right word but the use of the only word which really expresses what ought to be expressed. Stevenson sometimes it would appear to the superficial observer used the right word almost pedantically : Kipling uses the right word with an almost insolent disregard of the possibility of fallacy : Dickens used the right word perhaps not so much because he understood the use of words as because he understood the use men made of them. Belloc uses not the right word but the only word with such ease that it might appear to the uncritical reader (and happy is the reader in such a case) that the word had slipped in accidentally.

I refer to a later stage in the luncheon at Mrs. Cyril's when Belloc with a flash of genius coupled with, I am sure, hard concentration, uses the one word that describes the atmosphere surrounding the distinguished luncheon party. He tells us that the family portraits adorned the walls of the dining-room, but he does more. He lets us into their horrid and cruel psychology. Poor portraits ! You have been dead so long that you cannot expect to approve of the new generations whom you see violating all you stood for. So Belloc tells us that as the guests sit at table, they are sneered at by six enormous portraits. If anyone can suggest a better word than sneered I shall be surprised. I say, then, that Belloc is a front rank writer because he follows the great literary artists who have always known that the written word must be selected, dropped, selected again, passed in review, and finally when it seems both infallible and impeccable, adopted.

In other words the word " sneered " proves that Belloc has got into the minds of the six enormous portraits.

Those who are unfortunate enough not to know the inside of Fleet Street may be inclined to think that Belloc's newspaper proprietor Duke is exaggerated. Let these critics proceed to the inside of Fleet Street and they may consider Belloc's newspaper proprietor Duke underestimated. When the Duke gets rid of Batterby, the journalist who has dared for a moment to forget the news sense, we are shown a very true picture of the life of a journalist which, unlike any other life, will admit of no mistakes. Batterby has missed for his paper a scoop. Batterby, you inefficient little man, get out of Fleet Street, where you are not wanted. Get home to your villa and make up your mind that Fleet Street can do very much better when you are not there.

"'Batterby,' said the chief, 'did yer know about John K. ? '

'Yes, y'r Grace,' said Batterby, almost inaudibly.

'And yer didn't tell me, nor no one in this shop ? '

'No, y'r Grace.'

'Well, it's the boot, Batterby,' said the Duke genially. 'De Order of de Boot. D'yer hear ? ' He uncrossed his legs and turned to the table again.

The unfortunate Batterby tried to stammer out, 'Oh, your Grace, I understood . . .'

His master turned round like a barking dog : 'Git out ! ' he said, 'D'yer hear ? Git out ! ' And Batterby got out, still humbly, and went through the luxurious little corridor, past the outer office, stumbled down the broad dirty stone steps of the place ; he was as near tears as a man of his age can be. He wondered how he would dare to face the little house in Golders Green. It was ten o'clock."

A few minutes later there is an even more delicious sketch of Belloc's newspaper proprietor Duke—the great N.P.D.—shaking Fleet Street with his terrible limousine, his frightful overcoat, his fearful cigar. The conversation between Belloc's N.P.D. and the shrivelled up little secretary (a good secretary must first learn to shrivel) is even more true than the preceding scene with the N.P.D.

" ' It's a scoop,' he said bitterly.

The secretary shook his head : ' It's ruin and damnation ! ' Then he explained himself.

' Where's the scoop ? He wouldn't give an interview ; and just to say he's in London—what's the good of that ? '

' Lord, man ! ' shouted the Duke suddenly, ' doesn't he ever want a write up ? '

' I think he manages to do without them,' said the secretary drily.

The cigar was finished and the Duke threw it away. He handed his coat to the secretary without true courtesy, and the secretary, who knew exactly how far to go, held it for him while he put it on.

' The man's mad,' said the Duke as he struggled into the coat.

' They all say that,' said the secretary, pulling the coat collar down and valeting his master as in duty bound.

'They're ruddy well right,' said the Duke, and he stamped out to his private lift.''

Though I do not agree that modern fiction generally speaking shows careless characterisation, I am inclined to think that it does show rather vague characterisation. We find but few novelists giving the care to the creation of character that is, for instance, to be found in the work of Galsworthy. In light fiction there is not seldom an idea that so long as the characters are funny, it does not matter so much if they are inclined to be nebulous. Such a criticism does not in any way apply to Belloc. His characters are described in the best way possible, that is, over and over again they describe themselves. They are not, perhaps, exactly complicated characters : they are in some senses fairly obvious. But it is as well to remember that Chesterton has told us that the obvious is seldom seen. The Belloc characters are not capable of great emotion, but they are capable of the emotion which suits their temperament. Mr. Petre always gives one the impression, as he is meant to, of the terror of the man who knows that, though unwittingly, his life is a falsehood. Though Mr. Petre never knows who he is, he knows well enough that he is not the person other people think he is. In his false life he is somebody : in his real life he is nobody. He is obviously much happier as a nobody than as a somebody. Mr. Petre's confusion on opening a bank account with one of those deplorable people who sit from ten to four behind grilles like tame animals in the City is a masterly touch of characterisation. Belloc remarks that the bank clerk had a face like a full moon and no description could be more excellent of the people whose whole life is lived in learning that the one thing of no real value is money. Mr. Petre pays in a small cheque for seventy thousand pounds, and the moon-like bank clerk is so impressed that he wonders whether it will be fine for golf at the next week-end.

"The worthy young gentleman in round spectacles, mild, moonlike, but precise, turned it over, shot a glance at the back, pushed it back to the new-comer and said :
'Isn't endorsed.'
Mr. Petre looked at him with a vacant look of perplexed inquiry.
'Are you the payee ? ' said the humble associate of international finance, with just as much impatience as he ever allowed himself. But Mr. Petre boggled at the word ' payee.'

61

'Are you the person to whom the cheque is made out?'

He understood that! 'Yes,' said Mr. Petre.

'Do you want to pay it in?'

'I—I suppose so,' said Mr. Petre."

In certain ways both Professor Higginson and Mr. Petre proceed along parallel ways. Both of them get into a mess—Professor Higginson through his own fault, Mr. Petre through the fault of nature. Both characters invoke the Belloc wit, the Belloc irony, and, what is far more important, both give us the opportunity of hearing Belloc pronounce the various truths that are unusual in happening to be true.

Turning to "The Emerald" we find Belloc writing a detective story which is different from ordinary detective stories in that we know all the time who commits the crime as we are the watchers of the various villainies. Belloc in "The Emerald" is bubbling over with delight at the brilliant success of his fiction holiday.

The plot in "The Emerald" is the simplest possible. A valuable emerald is lost and many funny things happen before it is found. Belloc tilts at an ex-Home Secretary who is distinguished by the gentle manner and the invincible manner of the Government official. Belloc gives us a most extraordinary Secret Service man who, I am inclined to think, is more amusingly drawn than accurately drawn. " The Emerald " is, of course, much more than either " The Green Overcoat " or " Mr. Petre " a pure farce. In the hands of a less skilful novelist than Belloc this story would probably be both absurd and boring. As it is it has moments of intense mirth, the usual clever Belloc quips and a background of characterisation that is perhaps not quite so successful (except in the case of the ex-Home Secretary) as the characterisation in the two other novels discussed in this essay. We shall probably find " The Emerald " most satisfactorily by giving some glimpses of various situations in it, for as I say, the story has practically no plot except that the plot produces a successive story. The people who surround the ex-Home Secretary are, fortunately, people with money, for it is fairly obvious that they would be incapable of making any.

There is an incident realistically characteristic of the sort of people who surround the ex-Home Secretary when MacTaggart, an ordinary working journalist (and there will soon be none left) arrives as a guest. Miss Victoria Mosel, one of those women

63

who spend their whole lives doing week-ends in various house-parties, takes on a bet that journalist MacTaggart will pronounce the ex-Home Secretary's name wrongly. The charming week-end lady makes a bet with Lord Galton, a young peer who is quite well-bred and knows a foxhound when he sees one. By Jove, yes, of course he does ! Here is the amusing little scene written with delicate irony, showing only too truly that most of the hangers-on at house-parties are quite incapable of doing anything that is worth doing. Belloc in dealing with the journalist plunged into a house-party of county people is nearly as good as Mr. Max Beerbohm telling us of the notable novelist Mr. Maltby spending his fatal week-end with the Duchess's house-party. Mac-Taggart is hopelessly out of place, for the very good reason that a journalist is not inferior to leisured people and he knows only too well that they only want to "use" him. The only kind of journalists who are happy in house-parties are newspaper proprietors, and they are of course not journalists at all. Here then is poor MacTaggart at tea. How well we know his misery. There he is surrounded by the people who are only waiting for him to make a slip. There he is surrounded by these charming people who wonder at what Grammar School he was educated. Here he is in the midst of the select circle, not quite sure whether to be funny, whether to talk or not to talk, whether to cross his legs or uncross them. Altogether he is thoroughly out of place with people who cannot help being patronising.

"He was never at his ease with his social superiors (his father and grandfather had been mere soldiers ; his great-grandfather one of Nelson's captains ; *his* father again a very small laird in Ayrshire—but one had to go back as far as that to get to gentility). He dressed awkwardly, and he knew it. He never seemed to know quite where to put the hands and feet at the extremities of his uncouth frame. He also had a rather irritating trick of never looking anybody in the face. It was nervousness and came of writing too much. He was, I regret to say, terrified of women, but especially of ladies ; and he had already spent the first hours of his exile in wondering why on earth he had allowed himself to be over-persuaded and had come."

As "The Emerald" is a detective story, it is of course necessary to have a detective. Though I am inclined to think that Belloc's detective, Mr. Collop,

F

is slightly overdrawn, he is so amusing that we forgive the possible overdrawing. When, then, the Home Secretary meets Mr. Collop, we have some dialogue that manages to be slightly exaggerated and yet so amusing that we do not really mind the slight exaggeration :

"'Ah, Mr. Collop—it is to be Mr., is it not?'

'Yes, Mr.,' answered the gentleman solemnly, 'not Miss nor Master. Who ye're kidding?' He did not say it insolently. He knew his place. He knew he was talking to the Home Secretary. He said, 'Who ye're kidding?' by way of a respectful jest.

'Mr. Collop. . . . Yes . . . Mr. Collop . . .' stuttered the Home Secretary like a man half stunned. 'We had expected . . . ah! . . . you will pardon me? . . . a Mr. *Brailton*; yes, a Mr. *Brailton* . . . eh? Shall I . . . ah! . . . if by any accident there should be a mistake?'

'There's no mistake,' said the genial Collop, 'old Brailton 'twas to be! You're right there, Mister! But he was that sick he asked me to run down. "'Tis only a suburb job," says he. So here I am!'"

Perhaps the most ingenious part of Belloc's

detective story is the episode when Mr. Collop looks for the emerald so thoroughly that he tears up the floor with eager mechanical contrivances and tears down the pictures lest the emerald should be hidden within their recesses. Belloc is having a go at the Yard, not in a mood of hostility against its efficiency, but he would suggest that nothing is sacred to it so long as the crime is cleared up. Crime is engineered by vandals ; those who are employed to investigate crime are quite often worse vandals. Also Belloc is hitting at the lack of any manners which distinguishes modern police methods, much more in fact than in fiction. Mr. de Bohun may be the Home Secretary, he may wield all the prison administration, he may be able by his signature to send a man to the gallows or take him away from them, he may dine at Buckingham Palace and make the King shake in his shoes, he may even get courtesy from a newspaper proprietor—but in the hands of Mr. Collop he is but dirt.

" Mr. Collop's hand went up, and the blinding shaft of light disappeared as suddenly as it had come.

' That'll do, lads ! ' he said. ' We know one thing now any'ow. It didn't get down through the flooring ; that's certain. Now then, if you please, we'll open the furniture.'

Mr. de Bohun did not please.

' Surely, surely, it can be spared,' he begged. It's Victorian.'

' Now, sir,' protested Collop firmly, ' I'll be responsible for nothing unless I'm pursuing my own method.' "

And—a little later the same evening (if you will forgive a phrase that looks like a film caption), Mr. Collop hard at work while the Home Secretary tosses on his uneasy bed in the great room upstairs, indeed the only kind of room in which a Home Secretary could toss :

" It is a fascinating occupation to watch a powerful human brain at work upon some great problem—the face alive with mind, the tension of the muscles, the frowning eyes ; and to feel behind it all that driving, compelling power of the intelligence wherein man is godlike.

But no one would have seen this sight in the case of Mr. Collop had he remained. What he would have seen was a hand pouring out whisky for itself over and over again and adding smaller and smaller splashes of soda ; and at last an obese body attempting sleep in the lounge chair which it filled."

Belloc hits hard at Mr. Collop, but that worthy gentleman thoroughly deserves a trouncing. " The Emerald," though it has not the interest of " Mr. Petre," has a place all to itself. And it is that place which is occupied by all humorous novels—a place in the heart of the reader.

*   *   *   *   *

Though the background of Belloc's novels is a playground it is not by any means a bear garden. A certain stern morality as befits a Catholic novelist is to be found underlying all Belloc's work. He is not ever savagely angry with his characters : rather he does them the honour of putting them under the sight of his own mental microscope. He is all out against the vulgarity of the Press, the stupidity of fancy religions, the pomposity of officialism. One of the chief of his gifts as a fiction writer is his power of irony. He kills with laughter, as did Dickens. He destroys cranks by taking them seriously. It is the best, even the only way. Though the three novels I have discussed do not perhaps allow him the full measure of his brilliance as did " Emanuel Burden," they depict a courageous novelist. Each of the three stories has the most excellent chance of failure. Each has travelled along the narrow way, has refused to be led into ruinous digressions and has achieved success.

Mr. Belloc has given to the world a body of serious historical and apologetic work which the world, whether Catholic or non-Catholic, could ill have done without. He has made the writing of history the living of history : his essays on whatever subject they gossip cannot escape from being charming. Critics whose duty it is to suggest to authors as well as to criticise them would perhaps pay Belloc the greatest compliment by launching an attack on him—the attack of men greedy enough, discontented enough, to want a good thing and more and more of it. The publishers of Belloc's novels are right in their sweeping assertion that his novels make life worth living in these hard times.

For Belloc comes to his task of writing fiction strengthened by that broad and permanent sanity which underlies the mind which is both Catholic and literary. We do need to-day more than anything in the world perhaps fiction that can amuse, make a world that has almost refused to think, think again, and give it a respite, even if it be but a temporary one, from the savage and unseeing pessimism which has gripped many of our novelists to-day with a far more severe grip than the much more academic but, I think, less dangerous pessimism which seized the minds of Shelley and Byron.

At the beginning of this essay I suggested that Belloc wrote fiction as a kind of holiday. I am not sure that those who read his novels along the lines and between the lines will not find that his philosophy points to a sane, religious and sociological situation which would provide once again for the world at large not only a holiday from pessimism but optimism, leading to a Holy Day.

Photograph by Elliott and Fry

JOHN AYSCOUGH
(The Right Rev. Mgr. Bickerstaffe-Drew)

JOHN AYSCOUGH: PRIEST AND NOVELIST

JOHN AYSCOUGH: PRIEST AND NOVELIST

CERTAIN novelists seem to divide their novels into two kinds. The one kind includes novels which are interesting and important : the other kind includes those which are interesting but not important. It is a temptation in an essay like this to dwell almost exclusively on the former type of novel. It is a temptation which need not be overcome. The importance of a novelist does not lie in the number of his works or even in the versatility of them : it lies in the consideration as to whether the novelist attains to very high distinction in any one of his works. On this will depend his literary position and the judgement that is passed upon it by those who voluntarily or involuntarily make literary pronouncements.

John Ayscough wrote a considerable bulk of fiction. He wrote novels that were eagerly read and perhaps almost as eagerly forgotten. He had unusual powers of telling a story and most of his stories needed to be told. John Ayscough, I believe, would not have felt aggrieved at a judgement which divided his novels into two classes : the one class important and interesting and the other interesting but not important. The latter does not need the detailed treatment that must be given to the former if any real idea is to be gained of the scope, dimensions and range of Ayscough's works. It is probably true to say that as a light novelist Ayscough is as good as twenty other light novelists who can tell a story taking place in a circumscribed locality and society. His touch is light, he is able entirely to forget himself, he can throw himself into his characters even when they stand for everything that he stood against. But in the case of the really important novels that Ayscough wrote, he is in certain moods almost without rival.

I know that I am falling in line with popular position in agreeing that " San Celestino " is Ayscough's most considerable work. I am not sure that I am so much in line with a popular judgement in saying that his next most important work is " Marotz." Whatever may be the real value of the judgement which gives first place to these two novels, they do undoubtedly merit the bulk of attention in an essay which endeavours to consider to what heights of art and religious philosophy the subject of the essay attains.

There is also another reason why these two novels should call for special consideration. " Marotz "

is a psychological study of a girl : " San Celestino "
is a psychological study of a potential saint. The
former book is a work of imagination : the latter
is a work of historical imagination. It may be
perhaps said in passing that much fiction of to-day
which poses as work of historical imagination
descends to being mere work of hysterical imagination. Such a criticism would be the most fallacious
that could be applied to John Ayscough. John
Ayscough approaches the task of turning history
into fiction with the fullest determination not to
make the history fiction. Such a determination
will, I think, postulate two attributes in the mind of
the constructor of historical fiction. It will postulate
on the one hand a refusal to be afraid of reading too
much into history : it will postulate on the other
hand a refusal to be alarmed at the width of imagination that can be applied to history when the task
of creating historical fiction is in hand.

For what has the historical novelist to face,
particularly the historical novelist who stands for a
definite historical position ? Very generally speaking he will have to aim at pleasing two distinct
sets of people in two distinct ways. The two classes
of people that he will have to reach (and if possible
please) will be those who read historical fiction with

77

the natural criticism of the scholar and those who read historical fiction hoping that the history they refuse to read as history will be made interesting for them not as a fiction of history but in the form of historical fiction. And in the case of an historical novel of the nature of " San Celestino " there has to be faced, and if possible overcome, the natural prejudice of a population which is non-Catholic, without of necessity being anti-Catholic and also intolerant, possibly by force of circumstances, of religious experience it does not understand. In " San Celestino," Ayscough, I imagine, knew that his book had to face three types of criticism. The first type might say in so many words—You are not improving history : the second might well say— Why deal with an eccentric whom nearly everyone outside monastic circles has completely forgotten ? the third—a type of criticism based on a certain fear—might well say, and as a matter of fact did say— There is no propaganda so dangerous as that which shelters behind a fascinating story. John Ayscough replied with a perfectly frank and logical study of a saint who was as little understood by the greater world of his own day as he is by the greater world of to-day. The world neither understands sanctity nor genius, being quite obviously mainly concerned with the cultivation of all the things which only last while the soul inhabits the body.

There is all the way through the life of San Celestino that extraordinary mixture of humanity and divinity which characterises the saint. It is this mixture which ever infuriates the sceptic. He is infuriated at the divinity of the saint, merely to discover that he is tilting at a definite humanity : he is infuriated at the humanity of the saint, only to discover that he cannot catch up and smash his humanity because it is ever being absorbed into the divine. Ayscough, with all the understanding of the accurate and sincere historical novelist, does not consider that the portrait of a saint is any less perfect because it is an intimate portrait of a man. That is where the historical novelist can legitimately reach out further than the mere orthodox historian. History perhaps is too much of movements rather than of the movements of men. Historical fiction has often been too much the movement of men without due regard to the movement of history. Ayscough in " San Celestino " seems to combine excellently the movements of men not only with the movement of history but also with the movement of God.

Thus, when Celestino, the future Pope, though

for so few months, is but young, we have a most charming and delicate picture of the young priest-to-be meeting the carter and learning all too soon the sneers and laughter which is the world's eternal armour against the shafts of light which it hates because it cannot beat. Celestino finds thus so early that those who go to be priests must walk through a garden which bears the name of Gethsemane. The meeting with the carter is perhaps the first nail, and it is the predecessor of the other nails which were to culminate in the dragging forth of San Celestino to be so many years later the Vicar of Christ on earth.

" Petruccio blushed a little, and one could almost hear it in his voice.

' Well, but to-morrow,' he added, ' I am going to Salerno.'

' It is well for the rich who can afford such journeys,' remarked Biagio, interrupting his whistling but making as much noise as he could with his sieve.

' I am not going because I am rich ; but to learn theology, Biagio.'

' What is that ? It is a sort of grain I never heard of.' Petruccio laughed a little.

' It is all about God,' he explained politely.

' So it is at Salerno they know all about God. Well, I can't go. So I must stop here and remain ignorant.'

Biagio began whistling again. He prided himself on being disagreeable, and flattered himself that on the present occasion he was doing pretty well.

' You know I am going to be a priest . . .' Petruccio began again.

' That is right. You are not like your brothers. They are good for other things.' "

So true to life is the contemptuous suggestion that Petruccio is only going to be a priest because he is unfit for anything else. As a matter of fact he is !

It is but an instance of the accuracy of John Ayscough that the introduction of humour into the story of Saint Celestine fills its proper place. There are probably no men or women more possessed by humour than those whose life it is to be spent in the task of contemplation. The life of contemplation must of necessity sharpen the faculty of observation which is in reality part of the faculty of humour. It is indeed obvious that Celestine did have a sense of fun, it is equally obvious that Ayscough has given him the right proportion of fun. His meeting with the soldiers is just what would happen when a timid young man (already in reality a bold young saint) meets a number of rough men whose idea of a joke is to joke with a youngster clearly a bit " green." But Petruccio, even if he is going to be a priest, even if he is going to dwell in the caves with God, even if he is going to be thrust into the seat of St Peter, is human enough to laugh at his attempted discomfiture and turn round and get the laugh for himself.

" ' Where away ? ' one of them asked him.

' To Salerno.'

' *Lontano !* What for then ? To learn to be a doctor ? '

' A sort of doctor ! '

' He means a quack,' said another trooper. ' They are mostly that.'

' I have a broken heart,' cried another, who was good-looking and dandified, and put on a languishing air. ' Can you mend it ? '

' You see, I have not learned yet. Have patience a year or two ! '

' It will be broken again by then,' said a comrade

of the broken-hearted one. ' It breaks once a month or so.'

' Then he must know the cure himself,' declared Petruccio. They laughed at this, and said the lad would make a good doctor."

Not much later on Petruccio is treated by the soldiers as a leader. From endeavouring to make game of him, they endeavour to obtain from him a favour. Petruccio carries with him that peculiar air of distinction which seems to be possessed by those who are to hold high office and which is apparent to onlookers. It has ever been a kind of truism that future greatness can be discerned in the young. There is no truth in the French saying that every private soldier carries a marshal's baton in his knapsack, but it is true that every schoolboy who is destined to be eminent in after years has something of distinction about him, even if the distinction be somewhat modified by his refusal to occupy anything but the lowest place in the class. Greatness is not thrust upon men : great office may be, which is not the same thing. So the rough soldiers see in their young friend some one who will in the future be the distributor of spiritual favours, the distributor of the gifts that are bestowed on the saints. The episode of humour that I have already quoted is equalled in accuracy by the more serious episode that is here given. Ayscough is most careful to show that, whether Petruccio is riding with the soldiery or hiding in the rough cavern so many years later, men cannot help looking upon him as a chief and desiring him as a leader. Already the young student is dragged against his will into the position of one who leads. It is the Cross that befell San Celestino, the Cross not of obscurity but the Cross that thrusts a hermit into the fullest glare of a friendly and hostile world.

" ' Little priest,' said the serjeant in his ear.

' I am not a priest ; not even a cleric.'

' Will you do a thing for me ? '

' If I can.'

' Will you say a prayer for me ? Only one little one. My name is Rinaldo. Will you say a small wee prayer for Rinaldo, once ? '

' Rinaldo, I will pray for you every day until I die.'

' And when you are Pope, will you give me a plenary indulgence out of Purgatory ? '

' When I am Pope,' said Petruccio with a low laugh."

Then when the soldiers have gone their way, when the long straight road is empty of human beings, then Celestino experiences that curious mixture of isolation and companionship which is the true and distinguishing mark of the contemplative. John Ayscough takes us along step by step, gradually, gently, for one step is enough, as it was when Cardinal Newman set out from Littlemore and found the path to Rome. Here then is the future Holy Father stepping along the narrow and lonely way that is the reward of those who shun the wide and dangerous paths that lure common men and common women who have not been called to be saints.

" Here and there a light crept out of the quick-falling darkness, a little red light of some one's home, but he did not now feel homeless and solitary himself, though wandering along strange ways, among the great and sombre hills, unknowing where he should lie at night. The air of the mountains was colder, but the chill at his heart was less ; though the soldiers who had been pleasant to him were gone, his own friend would never leave him.

' I shall always feel him close beside me along all the way,' he thought."

In all parts of his work John Ayscough never fails to make his characters scrupulously true to life. He is the best kind of realist. He is the realist who really does make realism give the real. Many modern novelists make realism give the unreal, so determined are they to be frank, untrammelled by any decency so long as they can be described as fearless and even sensational. But Ayscough draws his characters truly because he is a dialectician, a logician, one who refuses to believe that the novelist should make his characters agree with their creator just because the argument would be possibly more in keeping with the argument that the novelist would like to put before his readers. There is quite an excellent little discussion between Celestino and his friend Alfeo. It is on the old perennial question of monks and hermits. Alfeo puts the time-worn worldly objection, while Petruccio replies only too truly :

" ' If everybody became monks and nuns and hermits, the world would come to an end.'
' Everybody never will become monks, or nuns, or hermits. But even if the world did come to an end, well, I think it would be better than going on badly.' "

86

If Ayscough can draw Petruccio accurately, he can draw Alfeo with equal precision. Such a gift shows not only the gift of the novelist, but the gift of the thinker, the gift of the priest. For who can know better than the priest the material arguments which are always levelled against monks and nuns by those who, being essentially worldly, know least of the world? And Petruccio may indeed listen to the arguments, the objections, even the futilities of Alfeo, with tolerance and even satisfaction. For Petruccio and all the monks and nuns care not either for what the world can offer or for what the world can take away for their following is of One who said, " Be of good cheer, for I have overcome the world."

Very often people who do not understand the *raison d'être* of monasticism have been surprised at not only the amazing hospitality of the monks but also at their refusal to consider anything a waste of time except possibly the mere amassing of material wealth. Even those who belong to the Catholic religion are not without surprise at the monks' refusal to be too busy to be more busy. When Alfeo and Petruccio leave the monastery in which they have been entertained while on a walk from Salerno there is again brought out with great clarity by Ayscough the difference in point of view of the worldly Alfeo and his unworldly friend Petruccio. There is expressed a certain amount of amazement that the busy monks have time to extend hospitality, courtesy and friendship to two unknown and ambulatory students. Alfeo suggests that the fundamental reason for this courtesy is to be found in the fact that holy religion allows time for courtesy because (and Alfeo considers he is quite logical) even the contemplatives can leave God for the small space of a few minutes. Then there comes the penetrating retort, which could only come with full force from a potential contemplative, that the monks never leave God. That is, of course, a completely true saying. As a matter of fact, no human being from the cradle to the coffin is able to leave God, which is a little distressing for the big money magnates who think they have succeeded so well in doing so. Perhaps the supreme difference between the contemplative monk or nun and the worldly materialist who is of all men the most to be pitied, is that the contemplatives never wish to leave God; the worldlings cannot leave him, whether they wish to or not.

The two points of view which Alfeo and Petruccio express by their almost casual conversation display with all the force possible the extreme difference in the points of view of the illogical theologian and the logical Immanentist who (in the case of Petruccio quite unconsciously) understands as far as is humanly possible the impossibility of life unless there is a permanent and indissoluble interpenetration of God and man. So Petruccio expresses in his rather commonplace little remark what St John expressed when he wrote, probably from his exile in Patmos, " I am the Way, the Truth and the Life."

" When they had finished, the abbot and Dom Mauro accompanied them up the sloping road to the corner where Urban II's statue now stands. Alfeo was readier than Petruccio, and when the time for farewell came he dropped upon one knee to kiss the abbot's ring. Petruccio was nearer to Dom Mauro, and kneeling, he lifted the monk's scapular to his lips.

'Come again, both of you,' cried the abbot; and the lads, still bareheaded, turned away.

At the turn of the road they looked back: the two monks were still standing to see the last of them, as if it would have been inhospitable to hasten away.

'In holy religion,' said Alfeo, 'there is ever

time for courtesy. They can leave God for a few minutes to be civil to two poor students.'

The exaltation of his own music and of its appreciation was still hanging about him.

'They do not ever leave God,' answered Petruccio."

Soon Petruccio has left behind the busy haunts of man. Out—out—into the vast plain, out into the grey space that is the mirror of the plain. Petruccio goes out into the solitude of the Campagna, determined that from henceforth he shall hear but one Voice, the same still small Voice that smashed down the mountain-side while the fanatical prophets of Baal cut themselves and howled on Mount Carmel. John Ayscough gives us a lively glimpse of Petruccio's soul as it rides along the rough and uncouth road that the body follows. We have a glimpse of the smashing unworldliness that descends upon Petruccio as he literally rushes upon God, as St Francis literally rushed upon the leper in his dreadful whiteness. The description of this headlong rush of Petruccio, this headlong rush from the voice of man, not because the voice of man is an evil thing, but because too often it obscures the Voice of God, this headlong rush to follow the One who had not

where to lay his head, is pictured with true and
delicate harmony of words by John Ayscough.

"'In exitu Israel de Egypto,' he sang to himself, as he left the city behind, and came out on to
the weird solitude of the Campagna. Its grey
emptiness welcomed him, its unearthly silence
cheered him, its waste and starving poverty en-
riched him ; he wanted to hear no voice but One,
he shrank from every society but that of God, who
alone bore with him ; he loathed every possession
but that of him who possesses all things.
Here and there a shepherd, almost as haggard
and silent as himself, would give him a bit of hard
bread, and now and then, at a peasant's dark hut,
he would be given a corner where he might sleep
at night, on a sheepskin, or on the bare mud floor.
But even to them he seemed a fugitive, flying they
knew not from what."

My attempted tribute to John Ayscough would be
very incomplete if I did not mention his peculiar
and ironic use of humour. The humour of Ayscough
is the humour of the man who sees that in most
circumstances of life there is something that can
afford enjoyment to the humorist. It is, of course,

a melancholy affair when a man thinks that he has a vocation to a life of contemplation and discovers that his vocation merely lasts while such a suggested life is in contemplation. But there is an amusing side to this undoubted tragedy. In the creation of Lippo Ayscough gave us a portrait of a priest who could not bear with the extreme austerities that were meat and drink to Petruccio. Lippo is one of those people who live by good intentions. He loves beyond anything the contemplative life at a distance. To feed on cabbage is bliss while he sees before him an excellent plate of baked meat. He sets a tremendous value on his own life and is not prepared, as are all true contemplatives, to lose it that he may find it. Ayscough is quite fair to Lippo : he is not a weak character ; he undertakes more than he is able to fulfil. He is the type of follower of a great leader who will always show his zeal by trying to improve on his leader's plans. He is like the Franciscan who wished to go one better than St Francis : he is akin to certain Trappists who introduced such impossible austerities that the followers of the Order fell into a loose way of living. He is not content to follow Petruccio in his rule of life : he must try to add to that rule and create something which his leader did not wish to create.

There is perhaps no better example of the correct method of treatment of such a man as Lippo as that shown us by Ayscough when the learned and experienced bishop puts the zealous but superficial priest in his right place. Lippo is explaining to the bishop that in his opinion action should be added to contemplation. Such a confusion of thought has existed down through the ages : such a confusion of thought must ever be zealously combated by the logic of the Catholic Church. Lippo is officious and the bishop, without appearing to be in the least rude, gently rebukes him. Thus John Ayscough shows us how a leader of the Church deals with an impetuous, well-meaning but, if not checked, troublesome son.

" ' But other considerations besides those of health have weight with me,' added Lippo. ' I endeavoured to convince Fra Pietro that we should add action to our contemplation.'

' The Church does not expect activity from people who live on cabbage,' observed the chaplain with a laugh. He was extremely active himself, and did not pretend to live on cabbage.

' It is very unwholesome,' declared Lippo.

' Unless taken in great moderation it must be,'

agreed the chaplain, who was thoroughly enjoying himself. He could not help chuckling, and the bishop interposed.

'What form of activity seemed suitable to you in connexion with the life of a hermit?'

'Preaching——' began Lippo.

'That would not do at all,' said the chaplain.

'Fra Pietro did not readily adopt your suggestion?' surmised the bishop.

'He did not adopt it all. Fra Pietro is not a person very open to suggestions.'

'He has adopted mine,' said the bishop, 'but I have not ventured to make very many. I certainly never suggested that he and his comrades should go about preaching.'

Lippo had another proposal to make, and it was not easy to get it out. But he did at last contrive to make it understood that he would not be averse to so going about himself.

'I have no doubt you would do it very well,' said the bishop.

'I could show your Most Reverend Excellency if you liked.'

'Do you mean here?'

Lippo intimated that he meant there. The chaplain looked terrified. The idea of being

94

preached at there and then in cold blood seemed to him quite inhuman. But the bishop betrayed no alarm. A danger that one has the power of averting can never be redoubtable.

' Well, no,' he said. ' The better you preached, the more personal it would seem to Messer Federigo and me. Let us take your powers for granted. Unfortunately we have preachers enough ; it is practice we are in want of.' "

And Lippo is like most of us, whether laymen or priests—he is not content that his powers should be taken for granted. But we must take them for such and pass on to the supreme day when the call comes to Petruccio to be the head of the Church on earth.

✳　　✳　　✳　　✳　　✳

It would have been extremely easy when writing of the sensational episode of Petruccio's election to be Pope to give either an exaggerated or an under-estimated picture of the effect of the most unexpected news on the hermit. Ayscough, with the true sense of the novelist who knows that the art of the novelist though elastic can break, does not fall into either of these mistakes. He is always able to have the subject well in hand. While Ayscough is not afraid of drama, he does not allow his drama to get away from his control and rant in a corner with the unenlightened but nevertheless enthusiastic plaudits of the gallery sounding their uncritical and unthinking praise. He is never in the vulgar sense a noisy novelist.

There can probably be no greater moment than the moment in which a man steps from a human relationship with man into a very special relationship with God. Petruccio might well be shocked, bewildered, alarmed, at the magnitude, the magnificence, the holiness of the office thrust upon him. He is called upon to assume the highest office in the world—an office founded not by man but by God himself. Had Petruccio been asked to be Archbishop of Canterbury he might merely have smiled at such a request, for the gifts of scholarship and learning that usually take the place of deep spirituality in the Anglican Church are not of sufficient merit in the Papacy. All the offices in the Protestant Churches are non-supernatural : the highest office in the Catholic Church can only be filled by a man filled with God. The tremendous shrinking of Petruccio, the hermit, from his colossal and even terrible call is, as I have suggested already, described by John Ayscough with truth, sympathy and judgement. Cardinal Colonna places the great ring of the Papal office on to the finger of Petruccio, and from henceforth while he is Pope, the finger that Petruccio raises encircled by the great ring is none other than the finger of God.

" Cardinal Colonna still held fast the hermit's reluctant hand. For a moment he loosed it, and under his red robe drew the ring from his own finger, then took hold of it again.

' We have a Pope,' he said, thrusting the great ring on Petruccio's finger. ' The Conclave is dissolved after choosing a Pope by acclamation, unanimously. The voice of God has spoken. I come to salute your Holiness.'

With a loud and exceeding bitter cry the hermit started back ; it was too cruel to be true. The cave grew black, as in the smothering night, and a rushing noise whirled through his ears ; he grew deadly sick, and his heart felt like lead within him. His tongue was dry and clave to his mouth, refusing to make words for him. He pressed his shaking hands to his eyes to shut out the darkness. Through them burning tears oozed out. He swayed, and would have fallen had Colonna not held him compassionately.

H

' Santo Padre,' he urged, his own eyes streaming with pitying tears, ' it is God's will.' "

It is no place here to make any attempt to discuss the merit or blame attaching to San Celestino for his abdication from the Papacy. It is, I think, sufficient to say that the verdict that John Ayscough gives is that Pope Celestine paid the greatest reverence possible to Peter's Seat in descending from it.

And so to the last scene, written with understanding and beauty, when the saint, tired of watching, sleeps that he may awake and behold in Heaven the Master he had served so long and so patiently on earth. There is a gentle passing, and I feel that there must have come over nature that same stillness of tragedy and joy which, as Mr. Chesterton tells us, came over nature when the spirit of St Francis which had held the whole world moved quietly from its earthly home.

" ' Laudate eum in psalterio et cithara.' Celestine remembered Alfeo's lute, and how he had flung it into the sea at last, to make divine music out of no other instrument than his own soul.

'Laudate eum in cymbalis benesonantibus.'
Celestine's ear brought back out of the far past
the music he had heard that day at Cava, in the
great church where so many saints lay listening
from their tombs. And, out of the future into
which the present was merging, a diviner music
gathered. Well tuned, indeed, were those cymbals, gentler than the stirred leaves of the forest
when the spring breeze touches them, sweeter
than the song of any bird, more delicate than the
chime of bells of flowers that only angels' ears
can hear.

'Praise Him on cymbals of jubilation . . .'
cried Maurizio, his eyes fastened on his master's
face.

'Omnis spiritus laudet Dominum!' Celestine's
voice grew strong in the last response of his last
psalm on earth. 'Let every spirit praise the
Lord.'

He said the Gloria at the end too—but not
there. While Maurizio was saying it in the cell
Celestine was pouring it out with a new unfalter-
ing voice in heaven."

And we who struggle so hesitatingly, so feebly, in
the outer darkness, whisper to him who dwells in

the inner light, " *San Celestino, Santo Padre, ora pro nobis.*" And in the gathering light surely we may hear, though afar off, " *Dominus vobiscum.*"

*   *   *   *   *

I do not think that it is subjecting the novel " Marotz " to any violent process to deal in some detail with the phase in her peculiar life in which this Sicilian girl is the inmate of a convent. For the episode is both important from the point of view of the further determination of the range of Ayscough's versatility as a novelist as well as from its own intrinsic value. We live in a world which has a tremendous prejudice against contemplatives, whether monks or nuns. There is much very sound reasoning in the part of Ayscough's novel, " Marotz," which deals with her life in a convent. The man of the world whose range is about as wide as a suburban street hates anything that seems to him morbid. The contemplatives appear to him as morbid people and he would probably not be much the wiser if you told him that they were mystic people. Any notion that a man ought to cultivate the growth of his soul more than the growth of his body seems to him to be an exercise that can well be taken part in when it is obvious that death is not far off. We have developed such a world-wide system of materialism (not necessarily anti-theological) that instead of contemplatives being looked upon as normal people, as they would be in a sane universe, they are considered abnormal and even dangerous, though what precise danger there is in a life of sincere piety has never quite been defined. It is, then, useful both from the point of view of the particular investigation in this essay as well as in the more general investigation of this book to consider the contemplative nuns as they are, so reasonably set before us by the brilliant and penetrating art of John Ayscough, indeed in every sense of the word priest and novelist.

There is a somewhat popular idea which is distinguished by its fallacy and enthusiasm, no unusual combination, and which complains rather querulously that monks and nuns claim for themselves a special place in the heart of God. Nothing is further from the truth. No people are so cognizant of the fact that the dictum, " God is everywhere," is a great and lasting truth. When, then, Marotz discusses the question of her vocation with the Poor Sister we discover the certainty the contemplatives have that only comparatively few are called to be contemplatives. So true to life is the dialogue here written by John Ayscough.

"'My dear child,' said the Poor Sister, 'do not talk much about your vocation, except to God. If it were advice possible to follow I would almost say do not think about it, even, very much. Do not at all events think about it anxiously.'

'How do you mean, anxiously?'

'Well, I think I mean this: Do not be anxious to have a vocation. Be ready to do what God wants. It may be that you should not stay here.'

They were walking in the narrow, high-walled garden.

'Magister adest et vocat te,' said Marotz, quoting the inscription over the door that led out of the 'Extern' chapel into the clausura.

'I know,' responded the foundress. 'But He is everywhere. He calls all of us: but He is not here only, and it is not to this place that He calls all of us.'"

Then there is indeed a lovely description of what the Little Convent of the Reparation really represents. It is indeed the gate that leads from the vileness of the outside world, with its sordid and selfish motives. It is indeed the gate that leads to heaven after so short a time of trial that seems to the mass of humanity folly and futility. Thus does Ayscough give us a small but charming picture of the inmost soul of a contemplative nun.

" Marotz said nothing, and the old nun went on in her clear, gentle voice that made the girl think of a dove——

' This little house is a low porch of heaven to those whom God wills should wait here, till the golden gate opens, and we can pass out of this short twilight into the unending light.'

' Till the day breaks and the shadows flee away,' whispered Marotz.

' Yes, dear child—the shadows that the world's false light flings. . . . But, if any should come here, which we pray him should not be, whom he has better uses for outside, these high walls would be a prison, and our cells horrible dens of captivity. Do not *want* to stay here, Marotz ; only want to do what is right."

One of the marked characteristics of John Ayscough's treatment of controversial subjects in his fiction is his keen ability to see the other point of view. Now while it is true to say that the mass of people view contemplatives as morbid and unnatural people, it is also necessary to note that one reason for this attitude (not the most popular reason, by any means) is that the process of contemplation is ever the reverse of spectacular. In a crude sense it is not even active. It appears to be a kind of passive mental process which does not display to the rather ignorant and prejudiced onlooker (who, by the way, never sees into the heart of a contemplative) that tremendous activity, physical, mental and spiritual, which lies hidden away in the silence. This inability to see the usefulness, the practical use of contemplation, is admirably brought out by Ayscough when one of the nuns in the Convent of the Reparation discusses the fact that mankind sees the usefulness of the Sisters of Charity much more than it sees the necessity of the Sisters of Contemplation. Mankind in the mass is not impressed by the spectacle of quiet. It is more impressed by the " noise " of the Church than by its quiet. The modern men and women who seem to imagine that nothing outside the twentieth century is much good, interpret any kind of restlessness, whether intellectual or mechanical, as denoting progress. If you tell an ordinary modern man or an ordinary modern woman that the real progress of humanity is to be found in the world that lies behind the cloisters, you will be causing much more amusement than hostility. And it is easier to fight hostility than to battle against the quiet but nevertheless unbreakable amusement of the many. Ayscough writes thus of this question of the more popular appeal of a Sister of Charity than of a Sister of Contemplation.

> " *We* could all see that *her* sort of life does immeasurable good.
> *Anyone* could see that. No unbeliever attempts to deny the incomparable self-sacrifice and humanitarian purposefulness of a Sister of Charity. To see that much implies no great perception on our part. But the usefulness of an existence devoted to contemplation is not obvious."

And again the Sisters of Charity have a better chance of impressing people favourably by their mixing among them as they do. Yet here is the paradox : the Contemplative Sisters take a wider view of all human activity than the Sisters of Charity. I remember well receiving a letter from a monk of the Cistercian Order who lived in a Trappist monastery in Ireland. He wrote to me, " Contemplatives have a more real interest in the people of the world than anyone else." This position is well defined by Ayscough when a little later in the same discussion about the Sisters of Charity he writes this dialogue :

" Oh yes. We are very few and always live together in an interminable aloofness from the rest of the world. They are perpetually meeting other people, and by no means permanently associating with the same small number of their own Order. They change from convent to convent, and in each convent meet new companions. That should tend to make them larger-minded. Do you tell me to believe they are larger-minded than your sisters here ?

Indeed, no. No one could be more universal-minded than our sisters. The Sisters of Charity are always, after all, doing much the same sort of things, and on those their minds are bent. Here we have *everything* to think of."

Once again John Ayscough seems to understand entirely the mind of a contemplative nun when he describes so intimately that knowledge possessed by nuns that their way of life must have its full measure of the feeling of abandonment by God because they too are inheritors of a crown of thorns. They are partners in sorrow even as they become partners in glory. They are courtiers of a King mocked and stripped but also they stand and gaze, afar off there is the shouting of all the nations for " The King of Glory passes on his way."

" Dear Marotz ! we were not left without warning ; the crown of thorns is for us as well as him. The servant is not above his master. It is enough if the servant be *as* his master. There was the Agony in the Garden, and there was the loud and bitter cry, ' Eloi, Eloi, lama sabach-thani ? ' What can we expect ?

Marotz remembered then of what a King she was aspiring to be a courtier."

The story of " Marotz " breathes that kind of southern warmth which throws the mind across Europe to the exquisite land of Sicily. The sun-kissed island set like a jewel in the midst of the blue sea is, for most northerners, so far off that it cannot be reached except through the medium of a book. It is quite extraordinary how Ayscough, a northerner, has been able to get into the atmosphere of the south. The story is sad, but, like most sad things, is lovable. Marotz is in reality a failure, but her failure is never sordid.

Next to the story of Pope Saint Celestine V, I suggest that " Marotz " is John Ayscough's most considerable work. It is an intensely Catholic book in the broadest sense of the term. It would be quite impossible to read either " San Celestino " or " Marotz " without gaining a new conception and a better conception of the philosophy of the contemplatives. The gift of irony of a charitable kind, the gift of humour of a pure kind, the gift of drama of a reasonable kind, the gift of depicting tragedy of a human kind—all these gifts make up the fine art of Ayscough as a Catholic novelist.

It would have been pleasant to have written even shortly on the charming story of " Jacqueline," the society girl who, not surprisingly, has no vocation to a convent. It would have been but dealing with another aspect of Ayscough's genius to have examined even with the necessary cursory examination of the literary critic who is bound by reason of his art to write pages on books instead of, as he would wish, books on pages, that really magnificent romance something like the broad romance of Hardy's work—

I mean the strange and almost overwhelming story of " Hurdcott." Yet once again " Monksbridge " and its funny little community, to be found in any English provincial town which has lost all conception of a living Church and is content with the dead bones of a complacent and lazy Protestantism would have called for a little discussion. For in that charming little story there is a horrid truth in the paroxysm of terror that descends upon the superficial little community when the frightful thing happens and the scholar of a Protestant school looks back to history and prefers to be a Catholic rather than a thief.

And lastly, there is Ayscough absolutely at home with the form of literature, a deservedly popular form, the form of literature which is the short story, too good for the magazines. In that medium, had I been able, I would have picked out the tragic little story under the excellent title of " The Release," in which a woman goes down to the railway station every night for twenty-five years to meet the husband who should have come by train but was killed ere he could do so.

*   *   *   *   *

I have endeavoured in this little essay to give some idea of the art of John Ayscough, Priest of the

Catholic Church and Novelist. John Ayscough has but comparatively recently laid down his pen. We may think of him joined to the band of English novelists who have ever kept the art of fiction both pure and controlled. No bitterness entered into Ayscough's writings even when unfortunately the subject might be expected to postulate bitterness. Ayscough did not believe that the novel should be stripped of a very clear insistence on the truths which the novelist held. His message is of course the only possible message for a novelist who is also a Catholic priest. It is that in a world of new theories, new religions, new moralities, new philosophies, new racial understandings and misunderstandings the one true and universal Church cannot and will not change. The work of John Ayscough echoes once again the challenging and invincible charge delivered once and for all to Saint Peter:

" THOU ART PETER AND UPON THIS ROCK I WILL BUILD MY CHURCH."

A firm insistence that there is no other way than the Church built on this Rock is the background of all the novels written by the Grace of God through John Ayscough.

110

ROBERT HUGH BENSON

ESSAY NUMBER FOUR

ROBERT HUGH BENSON: NOVELIST
AND PHILOSOPHER

ROBERT HUGH BENSON : NOVELIST AND PHILOSOPHER

IN an Essay that attempts to deal with a very versatile and brilliant novelist it is possible to do at least two things. The Essayist with more zeal than wisdom may endeavour to consider, however briefly, all the books that his subject, with complete disregard of the trouble he would give his future appreciators, chose to write. Such a method has both its merits and its blemishes. Should such a method be adopted the result will probably be the picture of a mind that looks under such a process something like mincemeat. So there is another method and it is the one I have chosen for this Essay. A writer of the type of Benson is rather like a traveller. He takes a number of ordinary journeys (these are his novels which have a certain dependence on each other) and now and then (as does Belloc) he plunges into a kind of literary excursion, which is nothing more or less than an experiment. So the enthusiastic critic may say to himself—let me try and get at the range of the mind of the subject I am studying, not by delving into all the activities of that mind but by studying it when it goes out on a voyage of exploration.

The art of selection, with whatever care it may be done, can only expect to please the selector. More often than not the selector himself is conscious not so much of the badness of his selection as of the mass of material that might have been selected, material which he is not quite sure ought not to have been selected. Any selector knows that the difficulties of selection lie in regard to the border-line cases, the cases which seem after observation to demand notice, only it just happens that other selections are not border-line cases but are so obvious that even the most superficial selector would pick them out. I do not know what books a critic would choose of Benson's to show as much as possible of the range of his mind. I know which I have chosen and, what is perhaps more important, I know perfectly well why I have chosen them. Now whatever we may think about the work of the late Father Benson (and he ought to have remained longer with us) we shall not, I think, be wrong in suggesting that he represents three aspects of the art of the novelist. And I have selected three of his books which seem to me to represent as strongly as possible these three aspects.

The three aspects that I see are these. I see Benson as the psychological novelist. I see him

(and I am not sure he is not at his best in this) as the historical novelist, and I observe him (and no Catholic novelist can help being this) as a " conversion " novelist. What three books then represent these three aspects of Benson's art as a novelist ? " The Coward," more than any other book, shows Benson to us as the psychological writer. " Oddsfish " discovers Benson in his most delightful historical mood, a mood that gets us back into history with that kind of charming insistence which makes us quite sure that just outside the front door men and women are whispering that Charles the Second will soon be returning from the races at Newmarket and " oddsfish "—what better occasion to change the monarchy not by revolution but by the ubiquitous blunderbuss. Then that rather funny little book with its brilliant patches, " A Winnowing," which discusses something of the philosophy that lies behind change of life, that change of life which drives (there is no other word) a man into a monastery to speak in silence to God, or a woman to the religious life in which she may learn to look at her own soul and get to know that if it is to flourish it must become good.

Let us then think a little about " The Coward," a book which made people talk for the very good reason

that Benson had made them think, and think a little uncomfortably, that psychology had a disturbing trick of upsetting theories.

*　　*　　*　　*　　*

It cannot be denied that in calling his book " The Coward " Benson did not mind relying on the power of a title. In this case there was no need for a title to do anything in the way of apology, for Benson had produced a masterpiece, a novel which was to achieve fame, a novel which was to deal with a very delicate problem, a novel that was sentimental without having any of the bad qualities of sentimentalism, a novel that might quite conceivably produce a more gentle attitude to those possessed of that kind of temperament which leads to contempt and anger from the rather hard hearts of men and women who are fortunate enough to be ordinary in the sense of not being eccentric and inevitably aloof. " The Coward " is something more than a study of a boy who may be a coward, in the eyes of the world often is, it is a study of that rather noble and yet terrible commodity which is known as tradition, that quality which on the one hand leads to the choosing of self-sacrifice and on the other leads to a kind

of obsession which will not allow that men differ one from the other as the stars, not only in glory, but in weakness. Val Medd commits many " crimes," but the fatal one is the fact that the Medd tradition cannot quite account for him, for it comes of a stock that puts physical bravery in such a position of eminence that the question of the breadth of mentality is hardly considered at all. We can at once say that Val is a peculiar Medd, he upsets their traditions, he acts on impulse when a Medd would consider a course of action, he considers a course of action when a Medd would act on impulse.

For you see, as Benson tells us, so that we may be prepared for future events, the Medds have " produced soldiers, priests, judges, statesmen, bishops, clergymen, and the portraits of these worthies throng the hall and the parlours ; " but, of course, such an eminent family has not produced a member who may be a coward, such a fate has not happened before, and naturally these eminent Medds do not know a bit how to cope with the unprecedented situation. That is the worst part of our family traditions, we so seldom leave any room for exceptions to a rule.

Val Medd, like all people who are slightly

abnormal, is always engaged in the hopeless task of analysing his emotions. Over and over again Benson shows us how Val keeps on communing with himself with the result that his whole life is a perpetual conflict. He has a fall off a horse which refuses a jump. There is nothing wrong in that, is there ? Yet there is—isn't the refusal to jump something to do with cowardice or was it to preserve the horse from an unnecessary and dangerous effort ? Would he ride again ? Of course he would WHEN his thigh was better. Was the thigh a good excuse not to ride for a bit, was it a good excuse that might be interpreted as a slight pandering to funking ? So Benson lets us behold Val arguing and always not quite arguing to his own entire self-satisfaction. So again Benson lets us observe Val's reasoning with himself. It is really the key to Val's instability of character. Of course, the fall hasn't made him afraid, he is not going to ride because it is not fair to horse or man to ride when one has a somewhat severe strain.

" The fall yesterday was nothing at all, he had just been kicked off—certainly rather ridiculously —just because he wasn't attending and hadn't been expecting that sudden joyous up-kicking of heels as the horse felt the firm turf under him. Why, if he had been afraid, he would have shown fear then, wouldn't he? He wouldn't have mounted again so quickly, if there had been the slightest touch of funk about the affair.

You're . . . you're quite sure?

Yes. Perfectly sure. . . . That was decided again. He would go to sleep. He unclasped his hands and turned over on his side, and instantly the voice began *da capo*.

' You're . . . you're quite sure you're not a funk? . . .' "

That is the tragedy. Poor Val is never quite sure about anything while the Medd family are so certain about him. And you cannot expect a fox-hunting family like that to realise that the unexpected ought always to be expected even in a Medd family.

Apart from the very careful creation of Val Medd, Benson creates with great skill the unpleasant relations between Val and his brother Austin. The brothers dislike each other, and it is a sad fact that brotherhood by blood is no certainty of any real feeling of brotherhood. Austin Medd is a splendid Medd, he does everything a Medd should do and would do everything a Medd should not do so long as he did nothing in the way Val did things. He has a certain good-natured contempt for Val and Val thinks that Austin is superior in rather a beastly and arrogant way. The whole fact of the matter is that Austin is intensely ordinary and Val is intensely extraordinary without this allying itself with any marked talent. Here then is an admirable little picture of the two brothers having a silly tiff, the kind of tiff which is nothing in itself but means that two brothers will never really be friends. You see, if only Austin had been sensible enough not to refer to the injury caused by the fall from the horse, because there was some sort of connection with cowardice in the incident. Cleverly indeed does Benson bring out the rather petty character of Austin and the character of Val, which is always on a high watch-tower, intensely watching lest it should miss any slights even if they were meant to pass by. It is in the depicting of clashes between opposing characters that Benson is so excellent.

" He strode towards the door.
' Your leg seems better,' remarked Austin, outwardly still calm.
Val cast a glance of venom at his brother and faced about.

' My dear chap,' he said, ' you'd be howling in bed if you were me.'

Austin simulated a genial and indulgent smile with extraordinary success. A sound burst forth from Val's mouth, which must be printed ' Psha ! ' Then the door closed sharply."

We must go on to the incident when it is again not quite certain (except, of course, to the Medds) whether Val is a coward or whether he is just the victim of his own troublesome personality. We are in Switzerland and Val does not like the idea of a jump in the mountains which would be abominably fatal if it happened to be a bad jump. Benson very reasonably gives us a nice little problem as to whether Val behaves as a coward or whether he just happens to lose his nerve. Of course, the unfortunate part of the whole affair is that the Medds do not lose their nerve in tight places, but I say that Val is a peculiar Medd, in fact he is hardly a Medd at all.

Now it is a pretty evident fact that many people are not in any sense brave on mountains. Val was not. He did not like the sensation of looking down and knowing that one false step would mean an end and an unpleasant end. He did not contemplate with any feeling of equanimity the jump that had to be taken because there was no other way round. And so Benson makes Val lose his nerve and the accusation thrown at him is that he is a deplorable and arrant coward. Now is it fair that such an accusation should be levelled at Val? I think that Benson makes the accusation if not fair at least logical. Val has by this time given the impression to his family that he is a coward, or if we like a word that is not quite so permanent in its hopelessness, he is an out and out funk. That is the opinion of Austin Medd, it is the firm opinion of old General Medd, who is not more of a fool than are most retired generals, it is the unspoken opinion of most of those who know Val at all. But does Benson, who after all ought to know Val best, think Val a coward? I do not think he does, at any rate in this mountain incident. Cowardice as the reason for the non-jump is arrived at and the possibility that Val has lost his nerve temporarily (as a much more experienced climber might) is rigidly excluded because the Medds when they get an idea (which appears to be quite often) stick to it under every possible provocation that would make it impossible. Benson is at his best in the description of the pathetic little drama on the mountain-side which is going to remain as a kind of cancer in the Medd tradition, a cancer indeed quite inoperable and I am afraid quite incurable. The drama unfolds itself with all that skill which made Father Benson so attractive a novelist, so brilliant a descriptionist, so human a writer and yet withal so critical a philosopher.

" It seemed to Austin as an incredible dream. Nothing seemed real, except the biting snow into which his fingers were clenched, and the gaitered legs of the man who stood now in Tom's place . . . the tiny details within the immediate reach of his senses. . . .

Then the gaitered legs scrambled fiercely and violently. There was a movement overhead as the others shifted to let him come by, and then again the ruthless voice began.

' Do you want to be kicked over it, sir ? I swear I'll kick you over it if you don't jump. Stand up, I tell you. Don't crouch there. Now jump. . . .'

Again there was silence."

And then there is the delicious comment of the lawyer who washes out all psychology and never thinks about the effect of cold and height on a nervous and irritable temperament. Father

Benson even seems to know the mentality of lawyers !

"'But it was just funk—the Philistine would say,' observed the lawyer with the cool, detached voice known so well to the clients of the other side."

The conclusion of the whole matter is that Val's conduct on the mountain is not a clear and unanswerable case of sheer cowardice. I am inclined to think that Benson thought it was not cowardice but loss of nerve. Much further on there is the Rome incident when there seems to be no doubt whatever that Val plays the part of a coward when he refuses to fight a duel. Of course the whole affair is a little overdrawn, a blemish that sometimes is allowed to appear in Benson's work. It might be here as though Benson wanted to side for once with the Medds and let Val be really afraid for his own skin even if the preservation of that skin meant a still further step in the smashing up of his character. Val allows his brother to go and fight for him, and the duologue in the bedroom when it is time to start for the arena leaves no doubt that Val is gripped by deadly funk of the worst kind. It is in Rome and poor Val certainly shows no kinship to a gladiator, in fact, long before there is any chance of a blow he is beaten. Cowardice calls out to him " habet " and he is vanquished without an attempt to put up a fight.

Even if the affair in Rome is a little overdrawn, there is again a splendid scene when the two brothers are in the bedroom in the pre-greying dawn and the hateful spectre of fear smiles sardonically at the head of the bed. And Nero fiddles on while Rome burns up all the Medd tradition in Val.

" Austin turned again, and there was a new ring of severity in his voice.

' Val . . . tell me. You mean to say you're not going ? that you're afraid ? '

There was silence. The writhed figure on the bed lay still.

Austin came a step nearer and tapped the extended bare foot sharply, twice.

' Come,' he said, ' tell me at once. Don't tell me you're a cur after all.'

(For there swelled up in the elder boy at this instant all the old bitterness and contempt, multiplied a thousand-fold.

He saw here before him one of his blood that

was a craven and a weakling ; one who disgraced
the name that he himself bore.)

The face on the pillow turned a little.

' I can't ' . . . moaned the broken voice."

That is in some ways the explanation of Val's
curious character. He does not want to funk, he
does not want to soil the Medd name, but when the
climax is really on him he is not ready. He is probably cursed with very much more imagination than
the rest of his family and in his case the result is
what must appear to the bystander as cowardice.
Benson is on the whole quite fair to Val, though I
feel in a way he wishes he could have made him end
his life boldly without a logical smash to the accuracy
of his character. But it was not to be, and poor Val
dies in the eyes of all the world (some gaping
villagers at a fire), a disgrace to the Medd family, one
to be spoken of in whispers, one who failed out of a
long line of illustrious ancestors, a silly little tragedy,
just a failure in a rough universe that has no place
for the weak.

So here is the pitiable end and Benson, true artist,
has no intention of sparing the family or Val.

" For he was there again at the window a
moment later, mad with fear, dashing himself

at the bars, wrenching at them. . . . And then the end came, mercifully swift.

A great crash sounded out above the roar of the flames. A vast explosion of smoke, lit house high by a torrent of sparks and fire, burst out of all the windows at once. And when it cleared the figure was gone ; and the noise of a clanging bell grew louder and louder behind as the first engine from Blakiston came at a gallop up the drive."

Crash ! But this time it is the crash of an axe and in Whitehall there is a two minutes' silence, though it is not November the 11th but January and the year 1649. Crash—it is a little further on and at the Court of England Charles the Second rules with cunning diplomacy, while outside Dr. Titus Oates persecutes the Catholics and at Tyburn Tree the crowds watch with amazement the Jesuit Priests who merely laugh at death, and at the Court Charles takes tea with Her Grace the Duchess of Portsmouth. " Oddsfish," and Benson has with a gesture plunged us into intrigue and villainy which were the twins so loyally attached to the Stewarts.

*　　*　　*　　*　　*

I do not know that there could be a better writer for an historical novel than Benson. He is even able to be strongly on one side without being one-sided. He can get right back into the period he is dealing with and yet let us know that we are in the hands of both a fine descriptive artist and a critic. Benson does not lose sight of the fact that an historical novel is both a novel and history. He does not forget that its appeal has to be both to the novel reader who likes history and to the history reader who likes a novel so long as it combines learning so that he may not be of the " common herd " who merely read to be amused. I refer to the ubiquitous high-brow who is never content unless a novel takes him (or more often her) into the realms of controversy, and if it be religious controversy his (or her) delight is quite unrestrained.

I am inclined to think that in many ways Benson in giving us " Oddsfish " has given us a very charming and true portrait of Charles the Second, the monarch who could make his queen love, even when he thrust his mistresses in her face, a monarch who could turn in a second from playful wit to Stewart savagery, a monarch who would let innocent priests be hanged for an invented plot, a monarch who could speak a series of indecencies at a public banquet and yet understand that some men were indeed called to be monks.

The story of " Oddsfish " is of course quite a simple one. It merely concerns one Mr. Mallock, a young Catholic who has many confidential dealings with Charles the Second and is finally instrumental in securing the reception of Charles on his death-bed into the Catholic Church. The medley of plot and counter-plot which surrounds the Stewart Court at that time is shown by Benson with the fullest force possible. Very early on in the book there is a simply delicious passage between Charles and Mallock when Mallock offers his services to Charles and the king asks him with true kingly discernment (Court services are but seldom dis-interested) what wages he will require. The answer is almost as unexpected as the answer of Perkin Warbeck to Henry the Seventh—that to be his scullion were indeed wages too high for such a noble and even utilitarian calling.

And there is in the conversation between Charles and Mallock something of that Stewart mixture of insolence and charm which made men laugh at death and account little of it so long as the affec-tion of His Majesty was not diminished towards them.

K

"He seemed not to hear me. He had dropped his chin on his hand, and was looking at me as if he were thinking of something else.

'So you are come to serve me,' he said presently, 'in any way that I will; and you will serve me only that you may serve your master better. And what wages do you want?'

'None that Your Majesty can give,' I said.

'Better and better,' said Charles. 'Nor place, nor position?'

'Only at Your Majesty's feet.'

'And what if I kick you?'

'I will look for the halfpence elsewhere, sir.'

Then the King laughed outright, in the short harsh way he had, and I knew that I had pleased him. Then he stood up and I saw that he was taller than I had thought. He was close upon six feet high."

Indeed—the Stewarts could kick and then one had but to make a joke and they would kiss. Benson brings out over and over again this kind of implied tyranny—this kind of warning that to put no faith in princes or kings was specially apt should they be of Stewart blood. And yet who of our long line of kings has gained such loyalty and gained such treachery as those who possessed the magnetic name of Stewart ? How Benson does get us back to the age of real romance when Charles the Second had the throne and My Lord Essex cut his throat in the tower. We are sitting quietly at home, and then all at once Benson lets us hear in the far distance the beat, beat of horses' feet that move quickly, and in a moment all is hurry, for we are away to London and it is on service for His Sacred Majesty that we are bound. This is indeed the delightful atmosphere that Benson put into his historical novels.

" Between two of the verses, I heard on a sudden, over the hill top beyond the village, the beat of a horse's hoofs, galloping, but I thought no more of it. At the end of the next verse, even before it was finished, I heard the hoofs again, through the music I ran to the window to see who rode so fast ; and was barely in time to see a courier, in a blue coat, dash past the new iron gate, pulling at his horse as he did so ; an instant later, I heard the horse turn in at the yard gate and immediately the singing ceased.

I went forward and received from the courier a sealed letter ; and there, in the twilight I opened and read it. It was from Mr. Chaffinch, bidding me come to town at once on King's business."

There is in such a passage obvious skill of the right kind. There is the sudden smashing up of a scene of domesticity, there is the premonition of coming danger, the suggestion of " troublous times " and the implication that away in London Town lay danger, perhaps death, but ever like a great shining star the glory of service for the king not only of England but the great king whose chief servant and interpreter rules in Rome.

All the way through " Oddsfish " we are conscious of the hatred that prevailed in the days of Charles the Second against the priests of the Society of Jesus. Benson gives us a picture of this hatred without any attempt at glossing over the melancholy and deplorable attempts that were always being made to add to the hatred of the Jesuits by the finding of alleged plots against the king's life. It is not easy for a Catholic to deal with this phase in history without feeling inclined to use forceful language, yet Benson all the time remembers that he is writing history in a novel and it is not his part to do more than narrate the events as they happened. Naturally he brings out the unfairness with which the

Jesuit priests were treated at their trial, but that is history and everyone who takes the trouble to look behind the scenes in the days of Charles the Second can discover a tremendous effort to smash Catholicism in England by means of a very favourite trick of that time—plot suggestion. Even Dr. Titus Oates is not made more repulsive by Benson than nature had already made him. And it was a chance that some writers might not have missed.

It is with really remarkable power that Benson brings out the reluctance that Charles always had to any discussing of his conversion to the Catholic Church. Charles is so like the humblest of his subjects in this direction. He will not willingly discuss a change of religion because it will inevitably mean for him a change of life. And such a change of life will mean for him a devastating change in matters of conduct. With what profound skill does Benson make us aware that the Catholic Church does not make Charles angry, oddsfish—no—a Stewart will not be so plebeian as to be angry over religion—it does not make him dissatisfied, for after all there is always Her Grace of Portsmouth to soothe the Royal dissatisfaction—oh dear no, the Catholic Church does to Charles what it does for everyone sooner or later, it makes him UNEASY. Listen then

133

to His Majesty, uneasy that Mallock forces him to think of the Church against which the world will never prevail in spite of its vain and puerile efforts.

"' Well—sir,' he said. ' And what of religion ? '
' Sir, I pray every day for Your Majesty's conversion——'
' Conversion, eh ? '
' Conversion to the Holy Catholic Church, sir. I would give my life for that, ten times over.'
' There ! there ! have done,' said His Majesty, with a touch of uneasiness."

The uneasiness is indeed personal and it is indeed political. So strange a combination of these two considerations was emphatically a feature of Stewart times. If we would get back to the real clash between the Catholics and the Protestants we may indeed travel along with Father Benson. We may then witness the times when death for religion was better described as death because of religion.

Then again a little later on Benson shows us with full force the battle between the personal and the crown in Charles the Second. The king is human but the crown is eternal. The king dies, long live the king who cannot die. The king may sin but the crown can do no wrong, the king may prostitute his soul but the soul of the crown will emerge ever fresh as a new-born flower that grows in the warmth of the noonday sun.

So the king with true monarchical candour, that candour which perhaps allowed the head of Charles the First to fall with a dim murmur on a cold January morning, defines his dual position. If we would, as common men and women, understand the Stewarts, let us pause and ponder over the words that follow, so that our judgements be not too uncharitable.

" ' You think this is not a fitting place for her ? '
' I am sure it is not, sir,' I said very earnestly, ' nor for any country maid. Would Your Majesty think——'
He jerked his head impatiently.
' What my Majesty thinks is one thing ; what I, Charles Stewart, do is another. Well : you must have it. There is no more to be said.'
There is no more to be said."

And on a little further and in the far distance the hum of an approaching army is coming. Stand still,

Charles Stewart, for the army of death approaches. But even so the king will retire from his uproarious supper with a smile and a kingly flourish.

So insignificant an incident, merely that the candle which shall light His Majesty to his bedchamber blows out and there is no draught. But it is a warning and on the high walls of the Court is writing— " Thou fool, this night shalt thou prepare "—and His Majesty waves his hand to the gay company flushed with wine and loose talk.

" As my Lord Ailesbury had given the candle to the page who was to go before them, it had suddenly gone out, though there was no draught to blow it. The page looked very startled and afraid, and shook his head a little. Then one of the gentlemen sprang forward and took a candle from one of the cressets to light the other with. His Majesty stood smiling while this was done : but he said nothing. When it was lighted, he turned again, and waved his hand to the company. Then he went out after his gentlemen."

And at the final scene let us take one reverent peep. For His Majesty passes and just outside the Royal Chamber the King of Glory passes on his way.

The King of Glory stops and Charles Stewart has gone to that account which awaits both those who serve as kings and those who serve as beggars. And in the great chamber is dead silence, then a wail from the courtiers, for the king lies so still and James has taken to himself the Crown.

"It was all he could do to thank me; and I value that blessing from him, a penitent sinner as he was, with the Body of Our Saviour still in his breast, as much as any blessing I have ever had from any man, priest or bishop or Pope. As he lifted his hand off again, I caught at it and kissed it three or four times, careless whether or no my tears poured down upon it.

As I passed again through the door to where Mr. Huddleston was waiting for me, I heard the doors at the further end of the chamber unlatched and the footsteps of the folks—physicians, courtiers, bishops and the rest—that poured in to see the end."

And so Roger Mallock goes back to the monastic life, and ever as he sits alone there comes to him the vision of the king, rake, scoffer, penitent and withal one who could destroy everything but the

137

love that those who served him were forced to give.

It would be indeed hard to find a better picture of Charles the Second than that given to us by Father Benson. There is no absurd whitewashing, there is no unfair attacking. The king comes to us in all his complexity, we are caught up by his glamour, we are thrust down by his excesses, we witness his religious dawdling, we are the spectators of the medley of crimes and counter-crimes which surrounded the Stewart Court. And above all are we shown the fascination of the Stewart character, its insolent temper, its sudden gentleness, its suggestion of instability and treachery, its power for making men slaves and women mistresses. Father Benson is indeed in " Oddsfish " an historical novelist of a high order, for his history though wrapped up in a novel is never novel in the sense of being untrue. Rather is it perhaps novel insomuch as it is fiction and history so charmingly combined that neither of these arts suffers.

*　　*　　*　　*　　*

It is not perhaps so generally recognised by students of literature and others that the real genius

138

of a writer is often shown by his smaller books. A writer who has any claim to unusual talent at all ought to be able to make a great book out of a great subject. In "Oddsfish" Benson had a great subject and he made a great book out of it. In "A Winnowing" he had a lesser subject, the effect of a sudden religious conviction, and he made a moderate book out of it. Possibly the "moderate" book is from the point of view of rather pedantic literary criticism, a bigger achievement than the "great" book. Be that as it may, in "A Winnowing" Benson conceives very admirably something of the peculiar philosophy of conversion. No philosophy is so peculiar or so liable to rule or so liable to break up all rules. Jack Weston, a Catholic, in the sense that he obeys the rules of the Church as he would obey the rules of the Jockey Club, almost dies. He so nearly dies that he is quite certain that he has died. The result is not really a strange one. It throws him back with a certainty that one day he will die and what is more he will remain dead. And now here comes Father Benson with a somewhat puckered brow. "Yes," he seems to say, "a curious psychological case. One comes back from the dead, one who is a Catholic, and what shall the result be to him who was dead and is now alive?" Well, the

139

whole result can be summed up very quickly. Jack Weston suddenly realises that the Catholic Faith is true in a way he had not thought about before. And the result is not only conversion from a mechanical faith to a living faith but conversion to contemplation of value.

In fact, the horrid fact is borne to Jack's relations that such a living faith as Weston has now achieved is going to be abominably upsetting, especially to the little village in which he lives. It means that nuns from France will come and settle in a wing of his house, it means that the Catholic priest will have more power, it even means (and this is truly frightful) that Weston will give quite a lot of money to the Church. Oh, yes, Benson lets us know that this awakening to religious reality is really quite irritating to the lookers-on. It is especially irritating to the Protestants in the parish, for after all in England you ought not to do anything to worry the Rector and his wife, dear charming people, and even quite religious.

In " A Winnowing " the cleverest character is old Lady Carberry. She is intensely aristocratic, she is broad-minded enough to have one or two Roman Catholic friends, and it would certainly amuse her to have a Roman Catholic (if only they would not call themselves Catholics) to dinner, for "my dear, Roman Catholic priests are so cultured and I really believe they seldom get enough to eat."

One of the most delightful episodes in this charming book is when Lady Sarah, in spite of her title and her breeding, is not able to score off Father Banting. Lady Sarah finds that she is no match for the "funny little priest," and this charming lady, no doubt the best follower of hounds in the county, is beaten by the priest. And the priests always will beat society ladies who have quite forgotten that titles do not persuade those who follow the successors of St Peter.

Poor Lady Sarah leaves white with anger. Benson is so sorry for her, for it is such a losing game to cross swords with a priest of the Catholic Church.

So the result of Weston's death is found in the climax when his wife becomes a nun. The last few lines of the book give the key to the whole situation. There is the renunciation of the world by Mary and the broad Protestant toleration which is never handicapped by imagination.

"But her veil too was down. Was it possible that she had seen Mary's face for the last time?

Where were those two going? Ah! there was

another figure come out from somewhere behind the deal boarding.   Yes.

'Look, Jim ; they're kissing—with their veils down.'

Jim sighed tolerantly.

Then the grating closed.

Jim broke the silence in the motor five minutes later.

'Temperament, my dear girl, that's all. You must make allowances for temperament.' "

*　　　*　　　*　　　*　　　*

Several years have now passed since the world of good and healthy fiction was poorer by the quick passing of Robert Hugh Benson. Benson left behind him a large body of very notable work. I have merely been able to deal with some that I considered represented something of his powers both as a novelist and a philosopher. All his work breathed a reasonable and large philosophy. Definite conviction did not make Benson intolerant. Tolerance did not ever make Benson lean towards compromise.

As a novelist Benson perhaps deserves to stand higher than he is sometimes placed. He risked his literary reputation by always writing a good story !

He wrote for the masses and the masses enjoyed him. His philosophy peeps out from his writings the whole time. It is an insistence on the necessity of the Catholic point of view and it is a challenge to those who write that religious conviction does not in any degree make for dullness or prosiness.

The three books I have considered are, in my opinion, the three from his works that can hope best to show something of his range. It was much wider than an Essay of this description can hope to show. Had Benson lived longer he might have done greater works. But that is to argue from the " might have been," always the worst argument for the literary critic to employ.

Kindliness, and its attendant virtues of gentleness and strength stand out in his works. Description, that dear friend of the ready writer, of great power is at the back of all his fiction. Philosophy, that sweet counsellor of those who create religious fiction, allowed him to see other points of view and yet never waver in his own. Creation, that dearest child to the novelist, was in his hands happy and elastic. Tragedy and humour, those unwavering friends of the fiction writer, were in his hands as precious balm to be used as and when they should be best employed. Religion, that everything or nothing to the creative writer, coloured with the warmth of truth and conviction all his work.

The only monument that a writer requires is the memorial that builds itself from his works. Of himself the writer is nothing, he is but vanishing or vanished dust. Benson has vanished into mortal dust. Somewhere his soul lives. And we who would find it, as it was when it inhabited this Temple of the Holy Ghost, had best look for it in his books. And in return it will show itself to us, white and without blemish.

SIR PHILIP GIBBS

THE FASCINATING NOVELS OF SIR PHILIP GIBBS

L

THE FASCINATING NOVELS OF SIR PHILIP GIBBS

WHEN a novelist consistently achieves a rising success with each novel he writes, there may be several qualities which account for this pleasing and genial spectacle. Such a novelist may attain to this evolutionary success through a mere pandering to a popular taste which is not low, but lowbrow. Such a novelist may achieve a moving measure of success because he deals with a pioneer subject and smashes his way into hitherto unploughed literary ground. Again such a novelist may attain to the joy of continued success because he deals with a problem of tremendous importance to every reader he secures. Yet again he may find this unusual success because he dwells on some stupendous emotion in a stupendous way. Or he may be just a very successful novelist because his style is simply from its very start doomed to success, as some style, no matter how excellent, is doomed to popular failure or its half-brother, partial success. Such a novelist who attains to success because it is thrust upon him will I believe have several qualities. He will be a natural writer, he will be an accurate writer, but above all he will be a fascinating writer. Very well, then, let us concede at once that Gibbs is an evolutionary successful novelist because he is a fascinating novelist. Having then stated this *a priori* supposition it will be the business of this Essay to make a short investigation of this "fascinating fiction" which comes to us from the delightful pen of Philip Gibbs.

I have employed the same method that I used in regard to my Essay on Father Benson and have chosen three of Gibbs' novels which seem to me to demonstrate as fairly as possible both his fascination and his scope. All three deal with young people, and all three deal with young people who are modern in the sense that they belong to an era which has finished with Victorianism and an era which is much more dead than the pre-Victorian epoch. I start with "Heirs Apparent," for it is not only a Gibbs novel but part of the Gibbs philosophy.

In this philosophy we have more than a little of the philosophy of youth. Gibbs is dealing with the dissatisfied, the impatient, the rather superficial and certainly supercilious products which are disgorged from the Universities each term as regularly as clockwork. Gibbs is concerned with post-war Oxford, that amazing place where in the place of the

148

old masculine monopoly there is now to be found a gigantic mixture of the sexes which has made the place somewhat like a kindergarten school. And yet there is underneath the old Oxford spirit, the old reliance on tradition, the old contempt for the orthodox which drove Shelley out, the old smattering of learning which is swamped by the importance of sport.

But if any writer knows the Oxford of to-day, it is Gibbs. He even knows it as well as the old Tower of Magdalen does, the old tower which laughs on a May morning and smiles grimly in December when the cold winds race up and down the " High," searching out all those corners in the old city which collect every draught that there is.

In " Heirs Apparent " Julian Perryam sends himself down and Miss Nye of Somerville has been sent down. For these two have found that Oxford does not take too kindly to episodes that commence at Maidenhead and end several hours before breakfast. Thus Perryam tells us why he has " chucked " Oxford and his comments are worth a little consideration. Miss Nye with all the impetuosity of the Somerville investigator of syllogisms is somewhat incensed that there is in Oxford a policy of prohibition, almost a French system of " *interdit*."

To which Perryam (spelt with a " y " please and
of course Balliol) replies in this manner.

" ' I know,' agreed Julian. ' That's why I've
cut Oxford. Partly. It's a cramping institu-
tion designed to turn out character in certain
moulds.' "

I am inclined to think that Gibbs would agree with
this rather impatient sentiment, but I am also
inclined to think that he would think that Oxford,
though it made character in a certain mould, made
it in a good mould and a mould able to stand the blow
of life, if not the blows of life. And that is the
strength of Oxford, that it will never conform to
the vile code of the world which is always self first
and never mind the other fellow.

With a very great deal of care Gibbs gets into
the mind of the Oxford undergraduate. He shows
us what that peculiar individual does think about it
all, what kind of philosophy of life he absorbs during
the magic three years that his feet resound in the
old streets of Oxford. We see what he thinks of as
he strolls across Christ Church meadows, we discover how his mind is shaping even as his lips are
shaping exquisitely with an Oxford accent. And

this silly little accent, what enemies it makes in the larger world and yet how it serves as a link when men meet in the far off China seas or the much further off recesses of Limehouse or Balham. So Julian shall tell us what he thinks about it all, what we may expect to receive from the gentle hands of Oxford, what gifts she will bestow upon us when we pack up our traps for the last time, when for the last time the lamps burn low and the strange and rather terrible lamp of coming life is full of oil, and we must change our old lamps of Oxford and take on the new lamps that flare so fascinatingly in the great and lustful cities. Julian's father, naturally a little incensed that his son has "come down" without a degree, imagines that Julian simply looks upon the whole Oxford system as a fraud. Gibbs shows us only too admirably the undergraduate point of view. And if you say that Julian is a disappointed undergraduate, then I can assure you that many graduates, fresh with their firsts, say very much the same.

"'Not quite that,' said Julian, with impatient impartiality. 'One has a good time, of course—though it bored me stiff after a bit. One makes some very decent friends, one gets a bit of atmosphere, a little smattering of ancient learning, utterly useless but not unamusing, and one learns how to tie a decent bow, how to handle a punt, how to hold a golf club or a cricket bat, how to tip a waiter with easy nonchalance, and many expensive and agreeable tastes. Oxford stamps one with the hall mark of a social caste recognised by an affected accent, superior manners and the snob instinct.' "

And Julian goes on to say with a certain amount of bitter truth that an Oxford education is a handicap. Unfortunately there is a good deal to be said for this point of view, and it is so much the worse for the world and not so much the worse for Oxford. Thus Gibbs introduces us to that spirit of impatience which is invading post-war Oxford and producing in that city of learning a vast academic socialism which has its counter part in the ever-increasing Labour Movement which is enveloping slowly but surely every civilisation.

And now Oxford must be left, and if the tower of Magdalen has a sardonic grin it is her own fault. Gibbs has a remarkable insight into the world of journalism. That is perhaps not surprising, for the successful novelist may indeed take much notice of the less ornate sister—I refer to journalism.

Julian's father is in a sense a typical journalist. He has very admirably subordinated himself into the background, he is careful not to see too little and even more careful not to see too much. He is indeed the tool of the proprietor and who knows better than Gibbs how many of these tools make an excellent living and nearly lose their flabby souls in Fleet Street? If the "High" in Oxford helps to find the soul, the "street" in London helps to harden or embitter it. There is, indeed, a fine passage of arms between Perryam and his son, and it is Gibbs at his very best. Julian is grumbling that his father's private views do not quite coincide with his editorial views. That is not surprising. The man by his own fireside is not the same individual as the man in the editorial chair, and that is one of the blemishes of journalism, or rather the paid journalism which is indulged in, because it means a good livelihood and a certain position of power.

" Mr. Perryam coloured slightly and laughed uneasily.

' I have to carry out Buckland's policy. They're not my views. I'm not a free agent, old boy.'

' A bought man ! ' said Julian coldly.

His father started in his chair, and for the first time answered angrily.

' I don't like that phrase, Julian ! I'd advise you not to use it again.'

' Sorry, sir,' said Julian amiably, but not ruffled."

A little later on there is a glimpse of what young Oxford thinks of the journalistic life, and it is as well to realise that young Oxford is a little idealistic and that Fleet Street is a little entrenched in the sordid side of life. You cannot help it if you are going to give news to the public and Gibbs knows only too well the dirty backwash of the stunt press. Julian in arguing with his father (the grin on the tower at Magdalen is now a little malicious and even sad) puts the whole matter in a nutshell.

" Julian rose from his chair impatiently, with a sudden flush on his face.

' No, I'm damned if I do ! Not the stunt press, with its divorce news and fabricated lies and dirty politics and split infinitives and hopeless vulgarities. Not after Winchester and Balliol.'

' Why not ? ' asked Mr. Perryam coldly. ' Do you think we haven't Balliol men in Fleet

Street ? Why, I refuse jobs to them every other day.'

' Anyhow, I'd rather sweep a crossing, father. It's cleaner from what I've seen.' "

Does Sir Philip Gibbs think Julian a prig ? I do not think so. Julian is simply rather a sad little boy who is beginning to lose a toy. His little toy is Oxford and the horrid cannons of life are beginning to smash up the toy. But if Oxford is a toy, part of it is unbreakable. You may disillusion Julian as much as you like but you cannot destroy his courage, you cannot make him give in, you cannot drive him to despair because Oxford, in spite of its river-parties, its absurd " rags," its appalling cocksureness, buckles on an armour and the armour is just that amusing little word " pluck."

Gibbs gives us a picture of sadness. Youth comes into life going to do such great things. Sometimes it does these great things, but if it does they are not quite so sweet and pure as they had seemed.

We must leave young Oxford in the person of Julian Perryam and gaze upon young Somerville in the person of Audrey Nye. Audrey Nye is the daughter of an Anglican parson, and this Anglican parson becomes aware of the fact that he is outside the True Church. Here then we have Gibbs dealing with a problem that has to be solved by comparatively few people. It is the problem of conversion and its attendant worldly inconveniences. Gibbs is excellently aware of this " behind the scenes " problem, this problem that in so many vicarages and rectories dare not be solved because of the family.

It is, of course, bound to be a shock when a clergyman of the Church of England discovers that he is the member of a Church which has no direct authority except in so far as a human pronouncement constitutes authority. It will shock the parish which has been content with a Sunday religion, it will shock the rectory employees who will have to poke round for another job. Most of all it will shock the members of the family, the members who cannot see into the uplifted heart of the converted one, the members who have forgotten the question of St Peter on the way out from Rome. " Quo vadis "—thou Anglican clergyman. And those who respond can indeed, in this England, expect not only misunderstanding but hate. And of all probably the members of the family will understand the least, especially if their bread and butter is likely to become bread and scrape. Miss Nye of Somerville (the old tower at Magdalen is beginning to laugh a little indecently) gets her shock and Gibbs is dreadfully accurate in his portraiture.

"'Audrey, my dear, I'm going to tell you a great secret. A most joyous secret, though it will lead to suffering for all of us, I'm afraid, and especially for your dear mother. I'm going to become a Catholic and join the only true Church. I've been thinking about it for a long time. I can hesitate no longer. To-night I put myself in the hands of Father Rivington.'"

To which dear Audrey replies as only a Somerville girl could reply. For, of course, Somerville does not prepare for shocks.

"'Good God!' said Audrey. 'That puts the lid on everything. Do you mean to say you're going to chuck up your living?'"

Now Gibbs is a very admirable psychologist. He knows as well as I know that if anyone happens to be converted to the Catholic Church the scapegoat is the Priest. This is a natural assumption, for we are always more prone to look at the Instrument than the force behind the Instrument. Thus poor Father Rivington gets all the blame for " his " conversion when it is really His conversion. Audrey, with all the superficiality of the modern girl who mistakes a human agency for a Divine agency, blames Father Rivington and the priest gets to the *raison d'être* behind it all. It is really quite a cunning piece of insight on the part of Sir Philip Gibbs and recalls perhaps something of his own blinding vision.

It is, of course, Julian who receives the revelation from the priest.

"The priest spoke of Audrey and said, ' Splendid girl, I should say. Very angry with me, though.'

' Why ? ' asked Julian.

Father Rivington hesitated and then laughed.

' I thought you knew. She thinks I converted her father and made him leave the Church of England.'

' Didn't you ? ' asked Julian with a touch of hostility at the remembrance.

' Not in the least,' said the priest. ' I can't flatter myself on that score. Mr. Nye was like Paul on the road to Damascus. He had a blinding vision. I was merely the instrument of his reception into the Catholic Church.' "

And Julian's reply to this bit of logic is really quite delightful. Only Sir Philip Gibbs could think of such a perfect English reply, such a perfect bit of English insularity, such a perfect gem of a country deformed by the Reformation.

" ' A damned shame, anyhow,' said Julian. ' It's thrust the whole family into poverty.' "

" Heirs Apparent " is rather a sad book because it shows the gradual breaking up of boyish and girlish enthusiasm. And the world can be indicted for no more unforgivable sin. And at the back of all the stress and storm and the fret of post-war youth Gibbs feels that we can ask—is it well with the child ? And we may indeed reply: it is well. So let us be with Gibbs and raise our glasses to Julian and Audrey, and as we finish a bumper we may notice that the tower of Magdalen has now a pleasant and even happy smile.

" ' Here's to Heirs Apparent,' he said with a friendly tilt of his glass to Julian. ' May you soon come into your kingdom. — Youth's all right ! ' "

*   *   *   *   *

Throughout history man has been sustained through many temporal disappointments by the suggestion of a coming Golden Age. It is perhaps hardly necessary here to say how pagan and revolting most of these prophesied Utopias have been. Yet when all is said and done, they do point to a certain unfading optimism in man's equipment. They do demonstrate the fact that man is discontented not because of material oppressions but because of thwarted spiritual aspirations. They do suggest that his discontent is virtuous, and though Man has ignored the most obvious Golden Age, the Ages of the Faith, it is not too much to hope that he will, even in the far distant future, get back to the Faith which has been given once and for all time.

In Sir Philip Gibbs' charming book, " The Age of Reason," we are face to face with the great things that Science will do for the world when man comes to an age of reason. Well, we have heard most of it before and we know that man has not come to a new age of reason but has to get back to an age in which there really was reason. However, I am reminded that this is an Essay about Sir Philip Gibbs and is not an essay on the question as to whether the Age of Faith was the Age of Reason.

At the beginning of this book Gibbs is once more in Oxford and we are in the close confidence of a distinguished professor of Science, one of those nondescript birds who are of the utmost importance to those who have time for " little " matters of exquisite learning, those who are not too absorbed in the callous and commercial outer world. Let us take a glimpse of Professor Jerningham (I had almost thought Belloc had created him) as he walks just outside Oxford with a Somerville girl, and remarks in such a loud voice that " we had better sit up and get busy " that I suspect an eighth part of Oxford will hear him.

" ' If they don't sit up and take notice,' said Professor Jerningham, lengthening his stride, ' science isn't going to save them from another world war in which the weapons will be far more murderous than in our last little strife.' "

Of course it will not. For it is indeed a frightful charge against Man that he has used so much of his scientific ingenuity in the construction of destructive weapons of war and destructive weapons of peace. I refer to the literature of the materialists.

So Professor Jerningham is like all the funny little theorists who manage to shake with horrible violence all the wretched cults which grow up because man mistakes progress and the sometimes stationary nature of it. The paradox that often true progress is stationary is possibly worth consideration by Catholics and even more worth consideration by non-Catholics. I am quite sure Gibbs is sorry for the Professor, for the learned scientist is one day " going to preach to the world," and the world will be seven baldheaded gentlemen and three " bobbed " ladies in Bayswater who will listen with the greatest attention so that they may form a sub-cult out of which can arise a minor cult.

Of course, the Professor means well, that is his worst crime !

" ' Oh, Lord, yes ! ' he said. ' I believe in the religion of Reason. I'm going to preach it to the world one of these days. It's the only way of salvation.' "

162

And then Gibbs hits the essential nail on the head. For the young Somerville girl remarks after all the Professor's eloquence that she is rather keen on God. It was perhaps something of the same feeling which caused the philosopher to declare, that if there was no God, one must be invented. It is this inherent keenness about God which has ever made the Catholic Church the final appeal, it is this germ of " God Keenness " which has ever smashed the Rationalists and made them merely the embittered and disappointed leaders of those who would deny this innate " Divine " germ in mankind. As Gibbs makes Margaret remark—reason is not quite enough —it leads to the edge of a chasm and it dare not look over—it is afraid of man's natural nature and would substitute a reasoning being devoid of faith. Man is a reasoning being, but he demands also something that can satisfy his " unreasoning " faculty—in other words, his faculty of faith, his inevitable reminder that he is both mortal and immortal, human and yet breathed into with divinity.

One very noticeable characteristic of Sir Philip Gibbs is his genius for getting at the essence of a character. He fishes out the small but nevertheless gnawing worry which makes a person never quite enjoy life. He digs out the pleasures which make us

163

know we are dealing with youth. He is most careful in his delineation of Professor Jerningham's father. He delves down and up comes the old man exposed in all the nakedness of his small soul. The old man is like so many materialistic scientists disturbed at the thought of the non-existence that will quite soon come to him. He is perfectly ready to prattle on that death ends everything, he is quite cheerful in condemning the whole human race to extinction, but there is one snag. He does not in the least want to die because it means for him withdrawal from the ken of human vision, because it means for him a place behind a curtain, it means non-existence, though let it be said in passing—no one has yet told us how we non-exist. For if we non-exist we exist in a state of non-existence. I cannot conceive that we can non-exist in a state of non-existence.

The old grandfather, with all that frankness with which a very old man will confide in a young girl, discusses with Margaret, now, of course, Mrs. Jerningham, his distaste for death. Sir Philip Gibbs lays bare the soul of old Jerningham, he dissects it into ribbons, it is cut up with the two-edged sword of sympathy and pity. Gibbs is sorry for old Jerningham. To get nearly through life merely to wait for non-existence is rather sad. Especially as he cannot be sure that non-existence is not in reality a very deadly form of survival.

"'Tell me,' said Margaret. 'I'll keep it secret.'

He stared at her as though wondering if he might trust her.

'I'm afraid of death,' he said. 'Isn't that silly?'

She did not think it silly. She thought it pitiful and sad. She was sorry that an old man like this—well—getting old—should be afraid of death. She thought it was only youth to whom the thought came with terror. Cyril had been gloomy in the catacombs because that thought had 'discouraged' him.

'You see, I hate to stop my work,' he said, 'just as we're getting close to things—those atoms I was talking to you about. It's like falling off one's horse when the fox is in sight. I want to be in at the death. Silly, isn't it.'"

It is to the materialist who cannot see beyond the end of his own coffin.

And yet it is all a bit sad. We can never quite get over that last walk with the old man. The sun sank into the west and the wrinkles seemed to stand out in the dying day. We felt the coming of the night wind and knew that the chill in it meant more than it would on any other night. We saw the birds preparing for rest and guessed that for our companion the long rest could not be far off. Admirably indeed does Gibbs picture for us the sadness of the walk when old Jerningham discovers that ere there is another spring he will have passed on, as surely as the spring and summer pass into winter. And he has no belief that the winter will as inevitably pass on into the spring and summer.

" ' I shan't see another spring, my dear.'
Margaret was startled and sorry.
' Oh, don't say that ! ' she protested. ' There's no reason——'
He laughed sadly, staring across the Common, as though he saw some one coming.
' The old man with the scythe ! ' he said. ' One can't dodge him at my age. Threescore years and ten. That's the limit.' "

Yet again with what truth does Sir Philip Gibbs show us Professor Jerningham baffled by life. He

is sure that all will be well when the world employs
Eugenics. Yet his baby is born dead. He is certain
all will be well if only we can be rejuvenated, but his
father falls dead at a dance in spite of this rejuvena-
tion. The Age of Reason does not quite go according to rule. Poor Jerningham is forced to look again
at his theories, he is forced to admit that facts
upset his theories. No, the Age of Reason is not all
right because " man cannot live by bread alone "—
he cannot put his life into a human made fixed plan,
he is bought with a price and he cannot tell in what
manner he will have to pay. Gibbs is again dealing
with disillusion. Not so much the disillusion of
youth as the disillusion that lies in wait for those
who are certain that a thing has only to be old to be
ipso facto—useless.

" But it wasn't quite all right. That night
Margaret's baby was born dead, though she didn't
know until three days later, because of her weakness. It was Hesketh who told her and he was
very white and troubled. It was a great shock to
him. It seemed to upset his theories of Eugenics
and his belief in the Age of Reason as a cure for
all unhappiness."

We have so long been accustomed to expressing admiration for the exquisite descriptive powers possessed by Sir Philip Gibbs that we have been prone to leave on one side the essential melancholy that underlies so much of his work. It is the melancholy caused by a dual situation. On the one hand it is caused by the material disappointments that await youth. On the other hand it is brought about by the hard fact that the unconventional way, the road impatient of any " taboos," the path free from any so-called narrowing injunctions does not either lead to happiness or lead away from unhappiness. In fact, it simply leads to dire melancholy ending in suicide or an even more dreadful state of hopelessness. Some of the characters in " The Age of Reason " defy all the conventions. Let us be fair to them as they are pictured for us by Sir Philip Gibbs. They do not defy the conventions because they are necessarily loose or even perverted. They defy the conventions because they possess the absurd idea that youth knows best. And youth does not know best. The end of " The Age of Reason " is indeed a terrible end. Guy, the son-in-law of the Professor who sees a panacea for ills in an Age of Reason simply commits suicide because he finds that cutting one's own road is simply a way of cutting one's own name prematurely on a gravestone. This is the frightful climax of "The Age of Reason," and Gibbs does not in any way spare us.

"Margaret was listening to some message. She dropped the receiver and stood there like a spirit with the lamp on the desk shining on her white nightdress.

'Who is it?' asked Hesketh.

'It's father,' said Margaret. 'Guy is dead. He has shot himself.'

She spoke the words as though she were in a kind of trance unemotionally, and Hesketh felt his blood run cold. . . . Then it was not a dream she had had. . . . The boy had come to her. . . . Something queer! . . .

He saw Margaret sway a little and rushed to catch her, and held her before she fainted.

Cyril stood in the doorway in his pyjamas.

'Oh Christ!' he said, and put his arm across his face."

There always is something "queer" in any age of reason, and it is usually "queerly" wrong.

* * * * *

From these two books that I have been discussing it is a relief to turn to a book in which the young character wins through in the face of all kinds of opposition and proves himself in every sense " A Master of Life." Very early on in this fine story Sir Philip Gibbs presents us with one of those word pictures which made him the finest war correspondent that the war produced. Titus Harsnett is the son of a big manufacturer and he has new ideas about the proper treatment of employees. That is the literary background of the story and this description is the topographical background of it.

" As he got beyond the shops and the cab climbed a steep street, he could see into the valley where the industrial part of the city had been built. From thousands of factory chimneys long ribbons of black smoke streamed through the fog-laden air, and here and there, down by the ironworks, great flashes of white flame and cauldrons of fire made an infernal beauty between the black buildings. Titus Harsnett, who had an artist's eye, could not deny the beauty of it, grim and terrible as some vision of hell, but it did not comfort him."

For his mind is away in dear fair France where the blue sea gently kisses the shores as though it would like to tell France how it loves her.

"It seared his eyes, and he tried to thrust the picture from his mind by thinking of the little French town of Tarascon, where the girls were singing as they washed their linen in the sun-baked streets, and where all the houses were gay with colour."

In "A Master of Life" Gibbs leads us into the awful background of a strike. We behold the hate that the men have for the masters and the hate that the masters have for the men. The masters are shown up as an unscrupulous set of tyrants who treat their workers as machines and consider them merely machines to give the masters satin chairs and their wives satin cushions.

One quotation is sufficient to indicate how terribly realistic is the art of Sir Philip Gibbs when he deals with tragedy.

"'This is war,' said the old man, 'and it's a fool's game to feed the enemy. Not a penny piece will I give to these soup kitchens. If the people want food let 'em work for it.'

'We can't let them starve,' said Titus.

'Why not?' said Verney. 'It'll do 'em good.'"

There is here then dire and disgusting behaviour on the part of an employer and Gibbs is not slow to recognise it. Lack of imagination is always deplored by Gibbs and no little of the troubles that come upon his characters are caused by this irritating omission. Titus Harsnett, the main character in "A Master of Life," is finely conceived. He hates the unsought power that his wealth gives him, he hates it that his workers really hate him not for himself (that he could have borne) but because he represents riches, tyranny, calculating comfort, power and the freedom to make them slaves or mere "hands" at his will. And yet, as Gibbs would have us know, Harsnett is all for the workers. It really does hurt him that the grumbling shuffle of many feet on the pavement under his windows represents the noise made by those who depend upon him for bread, bed and everything that keeps the body from violently wrenching itself away from the soul.

Harsnett is an idealist and a sentimentalist. Only too well does Gibbs know how hard his way will be in life. Fool—does he not know that if his way is to be easy he must as a rich young man pander to the wishes of those who will accept him in society because he can lend money. He must be prepared to be patronised by beautiful duchesses with husbands quite incapable of doing more than spending several livings, he must be willing to conform to the old rabid conservatism of the other employers, he must allow himself to be fawned upon by the daughters of those fathers who care for nothing lest it be a money match. He must expect to be disliked by his relations because he has money and they have to have what he chooses to give them. It is indeed hard for a rich man to enter the Kingdom of Love. So Gibbs plans out his story and we watch with amazed interest the fascinating growth of Harsnett's white and clean soul.

All through his life Harsnett plays the game, and he refuses to take any part in the dirty game that is played all around him. Even his association with a married woman is clean and this very cleanness of it makes for him more enemies. But, as Gibbs shows us, he does not care. He has a stiff hill to climb, there are places where he falls back. Ever onward he goes, cutting out in the ice of popular disapproval, step by step. At last he emerges on the top of the mountain and the glorious morning sun breaks over him, he sings for his heart is merry, he

173

has the strength of ten men for his heart is pure, he surveys the vast panorama that stretches itself at his feet and there springs upon him the unshaking conviction that he has won.

So Gibbs leads us to that moment when Harsnett is a Master of Life not because he has two million pounds but because he has courage, love and unselfishness. He goes away to do his job in Life and——

" he is doing it rather well, I hear, and the public knows as much as I of this man's honest work as builder of garden cities which, after all, is not a bad hobby for a rich young man."

*　　*　　*　　*　　*

I said at the beginning of this Essay that Sir Philip Gibbs was a novelist who could rightly be described as fascinating. I hope that my journey with him in some of his moods may at least prove that this word was not an exaggeration. But he is something very much more than a fascinating writer of fiction. He is a novelist whom it is worth while to study. He gives some hard knocks at modern youth but knows that at bedrock it is all right. It needs moulding, and I am sure it is his firm conviction that the only real sanity in the universe is the philosophy preached by the Catholic Church. His message may be—that we must get back—that progress is sometimes stationary—that youth must not be too impatient—that we must not be too impatient with youth.

It is difficult if not impossible to find any real fault with Gibbs' style. It runs along delightfully with an almost callous nonchalance. It gets into the hearts of its characters and we receive a picture painted by a trained and careful artist. Though it does not do to " read " too much of an author into the characters he creates, it is, I think, pretty safe to say that Gibbs can be seen all the way through. He shows us the " mess " left behind by the war, he brings to our vision the multitudinous plans that are devised to clear up the " mess." He says to us with all the power he can : Why, you have not yet tried Catholicism, you have not yet put yourselves under an authority that is Infallible. In one of his excellent books of Catholic apologetics Mr. Chesterton remarks that we (the Catholics) are the people of England and we have not spoken yet. Sir Philip Gibbs says much the same thing, but he would add : stand in the way of the blinding vision which drove

St Paul to conversion and see what this country can do when it gets back once again to the Old Faith.

In England the Catholics in the Chesterton sense have not spoken yet. But the Catholic Novelists, of whom Sir Philip Gibbs is so eminent an example, are beginning to speak with the certain voice that belongs to conviction. We must indeed pray to them that they speak louder and louder, help to smash up the fiction that is leprous with evil, force the public taste to that which is decent and worthy of English fiction. The Catholic Novelists have a grave responsibility. Sir Philip Gibbs is a shining example for all novelists to follow, whether they be the unimportant writers of novels or the much more important readers who take so much of their pleasure and leisure in the reading of fiction.

SHEILA KAYE-SMITH

ESSAY NUMBER SIX

SHEILA KAYE-SMITH AND HER REALISM

N

SHEILA KAYE-SMITH AND HER REALISM

IF there is one distinguishing mark of our
leading women novelists, it is to be found in
the fact that they are very ardent members of
the advanced school of realism. Quite often their
realism is merely an attempt to show off, an attempt
to prove their emancipation, their contempt for
convention, their complete breakaway from the men
they so studiously copy. Now and then their
realism is disgusting and merely the effort to out-
strip the rules which have done so much to retain
the purity (not the prudity as so many imagine) of
English fiction. Occasionally their extreme realism
is excusable on the grounds that the complacent
need to be crudely enlightened. But there is standing out like a shining star the Realist who is a Realist
because of an intimate embrace with nature. The
embrace is so intimate and yet so controlled that
there is in response to it a harmonious blending, an
evoked response that is both enthusiastic and fearless.
We beheld something of this Realism in the work of
Thomas Hardy, dangerous and depressing as was
his arrogant deterministic philosophy. We discover
this genuine, and I might say inevitable, Realism in
the work of Mr. Galsworthy, his almost pedantic

attention to detail and his scrupulous care of action and reaction, all contriving to make him an artist whose painting depicts not only the scene but the soul behind the scene. As a rule I do not think that women writers have been very successful in adhering to an intimate Realism. They have been prone to rant or mistake Realism for mere indecent exposure. Some of our modern women novelists (I exclude the sexual sensualists who are merely dirt-finders) in their frantic efforts to be Realistic have simply succeeded in giving us not Realism which is a picture of real life, but Realism as they happen to think life is. The result has been that we have been inundated with sex novels which have this in common, that they simply prove that first-rank women novelists are as rare as first-rank women poets. Now it would be unfair in the extreme to suggest that we have not in the ranks of our women novelists several writers who can be placed in the first rank from the point of view of their technique. They can be relied upon to write well, they can be relied upon to give us a story, but they can also be relied upon to give us a good deal of overdrawn Realism. And therefore I go right away and risking the imputation of being called a " generalist " I say that Sheila Kaye-Smith is not only a first-rank novelist but a first-rank Realist and her employment of Realism has no blemishes whatever.

If there is one predominant characteristic of Sheila Kaye-Smith's Realism it is to be found in the grimness which is so large a part of it. Miss Kaye-Smith is grim for the very good reason that she perpetually dwells very close to Nature. As Thomas Hardy made Dorset his own, so Miss Kaye-Smith has caught up Sussex and made that lovely county with all its charm and cruelty her most intimate friend. Her Realism is of the kind that only the country can really produce. The hardness of the soil, the bare sweep of the restless downs, the men and women who live by the turning of the soil are hers. She knows that the hardness, the grimness of the country is indeed different from the hardness, the grimness of the towns. The hardness of the country is more than anything else physical, but the hardness of the town is mental and even in many ways artificial.

It is far from easy to make any selection from the works of Sheila Kaye-Smith which can be said to display in some small measure her genius. It is obviously better to seek for her most outstanding characteristic and this is, in my opinion, her magnificent Realism. I have therefore chosen three of her books which deal with Realism and Sussex when the two coincide with each other. To consider first " Sussex Gorse " and then " Joanna Godden " is to discover Sheila Kaye-Smith dealing with tragedy as it affects a hard man and a hard woman. Then if we consider " The Tramping Methodist " we have a little insight into the question of conversion, that question which has now driven Miss Kaye-Smith into the Catholic Church.

In " Sussex Gorse " we are face to face with a man with a fixed idea. Nothing is more terrible, no state of being is so relentless. Let us get a fixed idea of the most absurd kind, perchance that we cannot travel by omnibus, and we are certainly doomed. Sheila Kaye-Smith in " Sussex Gorse " has succeeded in doing what so few novelists succeed in doing. She has created a character who simply astonishes us by his unreason and amazes by his reason. Reuben Backfield, not content with fighting man, fights Nature. He will, come what may, get hold of this obstinate piece of moor, cultivate it and force its wildness to be amenable to the discipline of farming. Nothing shall stand in the way, neither the opposition of his family, nor the determined opposition of the moor itself. He will subdue it even if the subduing brings about his own ruin. Such is the background of " Sussex Gorse," this fixed idea, this unconquerable obstinacy that refuses to listen to advice, this " mulishness " which scatters the family and forces Reuben to say— you shall slay me, O moor, and yet will I beat you——

There is a tremendous consistency about Reuben Backfield. No sooner is his father laid in the earth than young Reuben asserts himself. What—they drink chocolate, do they, and it is expensive. What is wrong with tea, which is cheaper, and will allow more money for the conquering of the wild moor ? Sheila Kaye-Smith pulls us right into a domestic scene, and *hey presto*—young Reuben will soon begin putting matters to rights. Here then is the young master taking command of the economics of the domestic expenditure, and though it is " middlin' cold " and the wind cuts down from the great moor, we must make ourselves content with tea and sigh in vain for the rich warmth of chocolate at two shillings a pound. How Realistic the whole scene is, and surely while we read we must change our boots which are all clogged with farm mud.

" ' . . . Mother, how much did this chocolate cost wot we're drinking ? ' Reuben's voice made them both jump.

' How much ? Why, two shillings a pound,' said Mrs. Backfield, rather surprised.

' That's too much.' Reuben's brows and mouth were straight lines.

' Wot d'you mean, Reuben ? '

' Why, two shillings is too much fur farm-folks lik us to give fur a pound of chocolate. It's naun but a treat, and we can do wudout it.' "

Like all men or women with a set purpose Reuben Backfield does not care a bit what happens to anyone else, so long as his plans are put through. He will dismiss his father's faithful servants so that there may be more money to push through his scheme. There is certainly a terrible amount of truth behind the writings of Sheila Kaye-Smith and yet she is careful not to exaggerate. Reuben will get rid of the servants, but he will not expect the work to be done unless he works doubly hard himself. Reuben is so hard that his hardness is always a surprise to his family—he has a store of hardness which is wellnigh inexhaustible. As Sheila Kaye-Smith puts it so finely—

" he is something like a hard substance emerging from a hitherto obscuring shadow."

Reuben Backfield is one of those really " clever " people who make no attempt at self-assertion until it is quite certain that they are in a position to fight opposition. This Sussex farmer is absolutely unscrupulous; even his brother's blindness and madness must not interfere with his plans. He is determined to marry Naomi and Naomi may as well make up her mind that she will be the wife of Reuben. He will bend her to his way of wishing and if she resists it will only strengthen his determination. And yet, how brilliant a Realist is Miss Kaye-Smith —things never go quite right for Reuben. He wins and is beaten at the same time. He saves his money, buys some of the moor, cultivates its unwillingness and it turns round on him, spitting hatred at the puny man who dares to violate its centuries of wild unruliness. Reuben is even made to fear the moor, it is possessed of a devil, it leers at him as he plants his seeds, it scoffs at him as he fertilises it, it jeers at him with a mocking and inscrutable smile. So Sheila Kaye-Smith pictures for us with all her discernment Reuben in the grip of a vague fear. But, of course, the fear is quite ridiculous—how dare the moor try to fight him—he has won about the chocolate, he dismissed the unwanted servants—he has seen his brother (a possible rival) smashed and his eyes blasted and blinded and his brain maddened until the earth should take him gently once more to herself. But all the same he is a little afraid.

" A vague, a sudden, a ridiculous fear clutched his thoughts ; for the first time he felt afraid of the thing he had set out to conquer—for the first time Boarzell was not just unfruitful soil, harsh heather clumps and gorse roots—it was something personal, opposing, vindictive, blood-drinking."

The story of Reuben Backfield is the story of a downward path. All the time, although he does not see, Reuben is beaten. He wins an unwilling wife and yet in the end her death cheats him just when he most wants her. Even Reuben's oats are a failure. Sheila Kaye-Smith does not pile on the tragedy, the tragedy just builds itself up. We can see him getting worsted in the struggle, conquered by his own indomitable selfishness and the subtle hostility of the moor.

" Reuben's oats were a dismal failure. All the warm thrilling hopes which he had put into the ground with the seed and the rape cake, all the watching and expectation which had imparted as many delights as Naomi to the first weeks of his married life—all had ended in a few rows of scraggy, scabrous, murrainous little shoots, most of which wilted as if with shame directly they appeared above the ground, while the others, after showing him and a derisive neighbourhood all that oats could do in the way of tulip roots, sedge leaves and dropsical husk, shed their seeds in the first summer gale and started July as stubble."

Like so many men who see very much more than their contemporaries, Reuben suffers from a surprising want of imagination. It is a curious fact that the most imaginative in big matters are the least imaginative in small affairs. A man may rule ten cities with the imagination of a great statesman and yet be completely unable to rule his own household. Reuben can see ahead to the days when the great moor will be under his rule but he cannot see that his selfishness is killing his wife and laying up for him days of loneliness and sorrow. He can look forward to the days when his sons will work the moor for him and yet fail entirely to realise that he is driving them away from home by his harshness born of a criminal want of imagination. With his lack of imagination Reuben fails utterly to see that his sons will not at all necessarily wish to take part in the subduing of the wild moor. This is well brought out when Reuben argues with the well-meaning curate-in-charge and refuses to listen to the suggestion that possibly one of his sons does not want to be a farmer. He is far too much a son of the soil to see that his son wishes to be a son of some other soil. The soil indeed would certainly soil not only his hands but his soul.

"Then when the Curate-in-Charge had inspected the school he had been struck by Richard's clever, thoughtful answers, and had, for some months after his leaving, lent him books. Reuben on discovering this had gone over at once to the parsonage, and with all the respect due to a Minister of the Established Church, had informed Mr. Munk that he didn't want no nonsense put into his boy's head, and spades and spuds were for Richard's hands, not books.

'I'm going to maake a farmer of un, your reverance.'

'But he says he doesn't want to be a farmer.'

'That's why I've got to MAAKE un one, surelye.'"

At the end of this splendid book we are the spectators of a victory, but at what a cost. Reuben has won, for he has beaten the moor. But the casualties have been grievous. They have included his wife, his children, his brother and even all his years have been eaten up. He wins in time to know that ere long he must lie in the earth which he has ever been so near. The song of victory is but the song of defeat, Reuben has won at Waterloo, but the sun dies down on a dreadful battlefield and from the ground there stares at him the wreckage that has followed in the wake of his terrible ambition. We have grim realism in this book, and if Sheila Kaye-Smith had written none else we could not deny her her well-deserved place in the very forefront of English women novelists. . . . For a moment before we turn to " Joanna Godden " we must listen to Reuben's murmur of victory—listen very intently, for the echo of carnage in the distance is not a false echo but a true one.

" ' I've won,' he said softly to himself, while behind him the blazing gorse spat and crackled and sent flames up almost to the clouds with triumphant roars—' I've won and it bin worth while.' "

For the utterly selfish man counts it as nothing that all have been passed by so that his own ends may be served.

" I've fought and I've suffered and I've gone hard and gone rough and gone empty but I haven't gone in vain. It's all bin worth it. Odiam's great and Boarzell's mine—and when I die . . . well I've lived so close to the earth all my days that I reckon I shan't be 'fraid to lie in it at last."

*   *   *   *   *

In " Sussex Gorse " I endeavoured to make it clear that Sheila Kaye-Smith was able to dwell very near to the land. In " Joanna Godden " she dwells very near to the people. She mingles with the farming class, she knows what they eat, what they drink, how they make love, how they unmake it, she knows their trials and their joys. She takes us right into the homesteads, those firm Sussex farm homesteads where the food on the table, the potted meats, the cheeses (at five o'clock tea), the jams, the bread and the hot toast remind us that England may lack much that can be got in other countries, but she does not lack the talent of heavy and good feeding. How well does she know the habits of the people, their curious materialism at funerals, their funeral hospitality, their half-ashamed desire to honour the dead by melancholy and honour the living by a lively response to the good viands of the after-funeral table. Sheila Kaye-Smith gets down very deep to the heart of her characters in " Joanna Godden." I am not sure that she does not become more intimate with Joanna than with any other character she has created. She is much more sympathetic to her than she is to Reuben Backfield. Joanna is a woman and women have the harder time, and of course they make the most of it. But this Miss Kaye-Smith keeps to herself !

In a sense Joanna is rather like Reuben. She will rule with a rod of iron, but a woman's ruling is more likely to be bent. She will not allow her employees to take advantage of her sex by indulging in laziness, but she cannot forget that man likes a cup of cocoa in the kitchen. She gains an unwilling obedience from her workers and she is quite rude to the poor

little parson who is not even offered a cup of tea !
We can indeed see something of Sheila Kaye-Smith's
coming Catholic tendencies in her attitude to the
Anglican clergy. They are ineffectual, they dodder
along in a kind of dream, they say the right things
and scarcely mean them—they are shabby, they want
feeding and I strongly suspect that many of them
want washing.

She is really quite unnecessarily rude to Mr. Pratt
the Rector, for after all she might expect to be thanked
for giving thirty pounds for a new harmonium.
The Pratt episode is rather delicious, and I feel
sure Miss Kaye-Smith has one eye a little con-
temptuously on low church Mr. Pratt who does not
break any of the Thirty-Nine Articles because he
has forgotten them all.

" ' Oh Miss Godden . . . so glad to meet
you. I—I never thanked you properly last week
for your generosity—your munificence. Thought
of writing, but somehow felt that—felt that
inadequate. . . . Mr. Trevor, I've told you about
Miss Godden . . . our harmonium.'

He had actually seized Joanna's hand. She
pulled it away. What a wretched undersized
little chap he was. She could have borne his

192

gratitude if only he had been a real man, tall and dark and straight like the young fellow who was coming up to her."

Which of course goes to show us that Miss Godden had an eye for masculine perfection, and it was not to be found in the harmless Anglican Rector ! And it also goes to show that ill manners are quite natural to some people.

Again Joanna is very much like poor Reuben. She makes up her mind to get the son of the Squire, not a bad little fellow in spite of tuberculous tendencies, and he is almost caught. Death saves him and incidentally Miss Godden is pulled up short by fate in much the same way as Reuben. It is certainly hard luck on her though I am inclined to think that the marriage might have been a little difficult. I wonder whether Miss Kaye-Smith killed Trevor for this reason. Now this brings me along to a sideline in this novelist's excellence. And after all, the byways in fiction are the real tests. Sheila Kaye-Smith is extraordinarily good in writing death scenes. She creates an atmosphere that is neither sentimental nor strained. I noticed this in her book, " The End of the House of Alard," when she remarked that " The Lord has suddenly come to the

Parsonage " or words to that effect. When Trevor
dies we find Miss Kaye-Smith at her best. There is
the necessary solemnity about it all, there is the very
necessary humanity also. The whole scene is simply
beautifully conceived.

" There was a faint sweet smell of oil in the room
—Father Lawrence had administered the last
rites of Holy Church. His romance and Martin's
had met at his brother's death-bed. . . . ' Go
forth, Christian soul, from this world in the Name
of God—in the name of the Angels and Arch-
angels—in the name of the Patriarchs, Prophets,
Apostles, Evangelists, Martyrs, Confessors, Vir-
gins, and all the Saints of God ; let thine habita-
tion to-day be in peace and thine abode in Holy
Sion ' . . . ' Martin, it's only me, it's only
Jo. . . .' Thus the two voices mingled and he
heard neither."

And there is the bitter climax for those left and
the glorious fulfilment for those who have gone
on just a little in advance.

" The cold morning lit up the window square,
and the window rattled with the breeze of Rye

Bay. Joanna felt some one take her hand and lead her towards the door. 'He's all right now,' said Lawrence's voice—' it's over. . . .' ''

* * * * *

The death of Martin has a very true psychological effect on Joanna. It makes her disagreeable, sharp with her workers, overburdened with the necessity of doing something to break down the sad memories. Sheila Kaye-Smith once again gets right down to the mentality of the people. The peasant class who represent the farm-hands have no sort of imagination. They cannot see that their mistress's irritation is an armour against despair and the obvious reaction from a great and abiding shock. No, they judge by what they see, and they just manage to judge wrong as do all people who merely go by appearances. Joanna is cross, she is snappy, in other words the woman upset by her grief is " scratchy." The farm-hands do not like being scratched and they might, I fear, if you listened behind a door, be heard to mention the word " cat."

" ' She spicks short wud me,' said old Stuppeny, ' and I've toald her as she mun look round fur a new head man. This time I'm going.'

' She's a scold,' said Broadhurst, ' and reckon the young chap saved himself a tedious life by dying.'

' Reckon her heart's broke,' said Mrs. Tolhurst.

' Her temper's broke,' said Milly Pump."

No, Milly Pump, you are quite wrong. It is Mrs. Tolhurst who is right."

Apart from her fine understanding of Realism Miss Sheila Kaye-Smith has a very great understanding of dialogue, particularly dialogue between those intimately connected by birth. A good example of this is when Joanna and her sister Ellen " discuss " a certain amount of gossip that there is about Ellen's friendship with Sir Harry Trevor. A few lines are sufficient to show the naturalness behind it all.

" ' Have done, do, with telling me that. They only talk about me because I'm more go-ahead than any of 'em and make more money. Anyone may talk about you in that way and I shan't mind. But to have it said at the " Woolpack " as you, a married woman, lets a man like Sir Harry be for ever hanging around your house. . . .'

' Are you jealous ? ' said Ellen softly. ' Poor

old Jo—I'm sorry if I've taken ANOTHER of your men.' "

Miss Sheila Kaye-Smith is remarkably fair to Joanna Godden. She realises that in spite of her hardness and rudeness Joanna is all right underneath. Fate deals her a dreadful blow in the death of Martin Trevor and the shock colours most of her subsequent life. Her sordid affair with the young man she meets on the sea-front is, I believe, all part of her reaction to her sorrow. Joanna is certainly not vicious, nor is she even a flirt. In fact nearly all her squabbles with her sister are caused by Ellen's flightiness and indiscretion. Joanna Godden is a finely conceived character. Her inconsistency is perfectly consistent. She is an intensely modern woman in an era when such creatures were but rare. We have now become so accustomed to the woman who is a " born boss " that we hardly realise that thirty years ago such a person would be termed at least a nonentity if not an unnatural busybody. The excitement that she causes among her contemporaries is not in the least overdrawn. They look upon Joanna as something quite outside their " ken."

In this book Miss Kaye-Smith is of course

something of a moralist. Her theme is the difficulties that confront a woman who has to stand alone. Joanna Godden's cry of despair that she did not find herself created a man, sums up the whole position. She suffers from sex disability, a disability which even to-day is very strongly to be discerned.

Sheila Kaye-Smith nearly always manages to end her books on a sad note. And yet in spite of the sadness there is nothing of the hopelessness which so characterised the work of Thomas Hardy. Joanna Godden loses everything, but she does not lose her faith. She can look backward to a road littered with sorrows and mistakes, but she can look forward to the sun that ever rises in the East. So we will leave her at her bitter but not despairing climax.

" . . . There she stood, nearly forty years old, on the threshold of an entirely new life—her lover, her sister, her farm, her home, her good name, all lost. But the past and the future still were hers."

*　　　*　　　*　　　*　　　*

In " The Tramping Methodist " Miss Sheila Kaye-Smith deals with the question of conversion, that conversion which has now made her find her home in the Catholic Church. That this book deals with a conversion to Methodism does not matter, the impossibility of standing out against a clear call is at the back of every conversion and comes to light in this charming book. The appalling state of the English Church about the time of Wesley is well brought out by Miss Kaye-Smith. There is no exaggeration in the presentment of the conditions. The Anglican clergy were simply either men who cared for nothing but hunting, or men who just carried through the minimum of services in the most desultory way possible. Young Lyte, who becomes the Tramping Methodist, is brought up in a Rectory in which the situation is intolerable to anyone believing in religion at all.

" My father's office was almost a sinecure—there were only two services a week at Brede, and only one at Udimore and at Westfield. On Sunday evening my father took off the priest with his surplice and lived the life of a fox-hunting squire till he put on his surplice again the next Sunday morning. Clonmel was not a priest even in his surplice, but from week-end to week-end a combination of the jockey, the sot and the brute."

All of which merely goes to prove that a Church with no proper Authority is likely to be full of mere scamps who find in the Anglican livings a living they could not find out in the world.

In " The Tramping Methodist " Sheila Kaye-Smith relies on some of the ordinary attributes of the romantic novelist. At the same time her particular and compelling Realism is not by any means in the background. I mean she relies on some of the stage effects which would be found in a melodrama at the Lyceum Theatre. There is the villainous squire who clanks about and would certainly shout at frequent intervals " oddszooks " if he happened to be sober enough to shout anything. There are the somewhat conventional ladies, fair and faultless. There is the complicated plot which resolves itself into the necessity of marriage to the villainous squire lest the squire speak and the unfortunate brother of the lady be duly and properly hanged for murder.

But I should be indeed distressed were it to be thought that I considered this particular book inferior to the others. I do not. But I do say that it is not so unusual, it is not so typical of the brilliant art of Miss Kaye-Smith. It is altogether much more the kind of novel that we should have expected and got before the craze set in for the type of the psychological kind. It has imagination but not genius. It has fine description, it has moments of intense drama and moments of sheer beauty. But it has no fundamental character like Reuben Backfield, and it has no outstanding woman like Joanna Godden. In other words, any competent novelist could have given us " The Tramping Methodist," but only Sheila Kaye-Smith could have rewarded us with the two novels I have been discussing.

But there is beauty in " The Tramping Methodist "; there is fine blind faith, there is self-sacrifice, there is the study of a preacher who is not far from being a Saint. I give here an exquisite example of a passage of real beauty, that kind of delirious beauty that Stevenson sometimes falls into, that kind of whimsical dialogue that escapes so often from the mind of Sir James Barrie. So much abominable nonsense is sung and talked about the moon by artists whose only moon is a money moon that it is delightful to find the moon being discussed not only charmingly but reasonably. If the moon has ears, she must indeed have blushed at the lovely things said about her.

The passage is so exquisite that I quote it at some length.

" The moon was high among the stars, and the nightingale was drowning with his rich wild voice the drowsy twitter of some bird yet awake. We crossed the lawn to the shrubbery, and the roses that tangled the path brushed dew on to our cheeks. The spell of the night was upon us, and neither of us spoke for some time.

'I love the moonlight,' I said at last.

'I hate it,' said Ruth.

'Why?'

'It seems so cold and cruel; it mocks me. Why do you love it?'

'Because it is like—like——'

'Like what?'

'Like you.'

She laughed shrilly.

'How can it be like me?'

'It is so beautiful.'

She laughed again."

To go from beauty to sheer horror is to make but exploration into the power and scope of a novelist. When Lyte is thrown into the dark cell in the prison in which he is incarcerated on a charge of murder we are at the other extreme, and Sheila Kaye-Smith surrounds us with terror and despair.

Her description is magnificent and throws us back once more to her grim and relentless Realism.

" Oh, that dreadful dark ! It seemed to enwrap my very soul ; it seemed a loathsome material thing ; it seemed to crush me. I felt blood trickling down my chin. What had happened ? And I remembered. I had bitten my lips to keep down my cries while I was being flogged and they still bled. I longed to lose consciousness once more, for no phantasmagoria could be worse than the awful reality, and at last I fell into a kind of waking dream."

Once again a lovely passage brings this story to a close. Reuben Backfield and Joanna Godden have not much joy to look forward to, but for Lyte there is great joy coming. The sky is blue, the birds sing sweetly from its blue depth, for Lyte is to go forward with her who is chosen to be his helper.

" The wind lifted a sob, and swept upon us from the huddling fields of Kent, and blew a strand of Ruth's hair across my mouth. I held it there while the blast sobbed again—blustered—and was still. Far, far away, a shooting star crossed the sky above

Shoyswell, and I saw it sink among the woods like a burning eye."

*   *   *   *   *

It is not very long since Sheila Kaye-Smith became a Catholic. She has always been a potential Catholic. It is not of course easy to find in her novels an actual Catholic policy. But it is implied all the way through. Her irritation with the Anglican clergy of the Low Church type logically led her to Anglo-Catholicism; the next step was merely logic.

The Catholic Church may congratulate herself on having in her fold the best living English woman novelist. She is the best English woman novelist for the best possible reason. And that is that she has all the skill of the masculine novelist. Women novelists on the whole are distinctly inferior to the best masculine novelists. Miss Sheila Kaye-Smith is equal to the best of our masculine novelists. She has also that power of " creation " which has ever belonged to the great writers of fiction. She has that intimate kinship with tragedy without which it is impossible to produce outstanding fiction. Sheila Kaye-Smith, unlike so many novelists, is quite unafraid of letting her characters smash their own way along. She will not compromise and allow them to choose the easier path, nor will she allow them to whine that life is hard. For we know well enough if we take the trouble to study her fiction that they quite often make life hard by their own hardness.

Because I say that Sheila Kaye-Smith is the best of the English women novelists it is not the same thing as saying that she is a great novelist. Therefore I go even further and say that she is a great novelist because her characters are " great " people. They live with great force in her fiction, they are almost, not quite, great enough to live OUTSIDE her fiction. They are not quite so famous as Soames and Irene, for instance, but I believe that Mr. Backfield (I am not laughing at Reuben's pomposity in this way) and Miss Godden deserve to be.

We are sometimes told that English fiction is dying. In these Essays I have, I believe, proved that the reverse is the case, that our Catholic novelists are indeed Catholic. Miss Sheila Kaye-Smith has given us a fiction worthy of the eternal life of the Sussex countryside. Her characters rise from the soil and go down to the soil. Their passage is not an easy one. We are shown the journey stripped of all glossing. We have an intimate sight of strange men and strange women, we live with them for a few hours and they are gone. But we do not forget. Reuben Backfield, Joanna Godden, Mr. Lyte and even Ruth come back to us as we gaze at the sparks in the fire. They give to us the gift of memories. Miss Sheila Kaye-Smith allows them to parade before us. At the end of the performance we can but arise and give thanks that our entertainment, even our instruction, has come through the genius of a woman writer—not so very long up from Sussex.

KATHERINE TYNAN

ESSAY NUMBER SEVEN

KATHERINE TYNAN AND HER STORIES

ALTHOUGH Mrs. Tynan is a modern novelist, we seem to step a long way back in her novels. We are away from the novel, so popular in our own day, which is scarcely a story. We are æons away from any sordidness, any beastly eroticism, the backwash of so much of our modern fiction. Mrs. Tynan is not in any sense a great novelist. She has no place in the same rank as Sheila Kaye-Smith, she has not a masterly touch of creation, but she can give us a very good story. I do not want to be misunderstood if I say that Mrs. Tynan is more than anything else the type of novelist who gets a rather obvious but good plot. Sometimes we are in danger of forgetting exactly what a plot is. In so much modern fiction, excluding detective fiction, there is no plot at all. We are simply gazing at the map of a mind. But in the stories of Mrs. Tynan we are introduced not only to a good plot but to an exciting tale and a tale which is always perfectly clean. A great deal of the fiction of our era can be best described as perfectly dirty. Mrs. Tynan is clever without being in the least subtle. She is smart without letting her fiction become merely shallow smartness.

In the final Essay in this book I have purposely included Mrs. Tynan because she is so completely different from the other novelists written of. The six I have considered so far are in a limited sense slaves of the age in which they happen to live. Mrs. Tynan is not. She is an independent novelist who still believes that the kind of novel which has a melodramatic background can find acceptance in this age which is sceptical of anything it can easily understand. We have the old-fashioned attributes of the old-fashioned novel in her stories. We are really quite thrilled (or at least I am thrilled) by the awful thunderstorm, we are horrified at the walk in the blinding snow and the sudden realisation of the walkers that they are but a few steps from the edge of the cliffs, in front of which an angry and grey sea throws itself restlessly about. But I am determined to let Mrs. Tynan speak for herself through her stories, and we may as well look at " Denys the Dreamer," a really delicious story to snuggle into over a roaring fire.

In this book we discover Mrs. Tynan venturing rather near a psychological study. But all the time she keeps a good story going. Denys is a dreamer, and like many dreamers he gets things done. He is brought into line as it were by the mildly contemptuous attitude which is adopted towards him. It does not make him sullen, but it gives him an obstinacy which refuses to be beaten. Lord Leenane, who has as many brains as is compatible with a potentially bankrupt peer, has quite a good deal of insight, and soon discovers that the dreams which Denys indulges in are dreams that lead, not to a maudlin state, but to action. So we see a picture of Denys getting the impetus, and all the time we feel that Mrs. Tynan is plunging along quickly and certainly with her story.

" Leenane stared.
' I don't agree with Mr. Reddy,' he said, turning to Patrick Fitzmaurice. ' The boy's dreams are fine dreams, dreams of doing. Let us see if he can drain the bog. Do you hear, Dawn ? Denys Fitzmaurice thinks he can drain the bog and bring the cattle and the houses and the people. Isn't it a fine dream ? '
' I should like to see him do it,' said Dawn. ' Would the flowers go then and the bog cotton and the little blue butterflies like bits of sky ? The bog is a lovely place.'
' Oh, yes, please, do make a field of this little bit,' cried Dawn.

' I'll try to,' said Denys, very straight and his eyes like agates."

The whole story of Denys centres round his life as agent to Lord Leenane. Sometimes in true novelist fashion, Mrs. Tynan exaggerates. She creates in a somewhat superficial manner a philanthropic moneylender and possibly her creation is absurd. At the same time Mr. Aarons is a rather interesting moneylender and his wife is even more intriguing. Denys of course is attracted to Mrs. Aarons, and this is all as it should be in a novel which is obviously written to attract the masses, Denys in the company of Mrs. Aarons goes a small round of exclusive London, and we certainly get some sly peeps at life in society which lives on the right side of Grosvenor Square. There is a really charming little scene when Denys, landed at a big reception, finds himself talking to the type of old lady who can tell you where Queen Victoria bought her bonnets and why Mr. Gladstone did whatever he happened to do. Mrs. Tynan does certainly deal very truly with the sort of conversation which ensues when a famous lady, now well past eighty and a little deaf, amuses herself by two or three minutes' chat with a youngster. The funny old lady is a dear old lady, and if you sit very quietly in Rotten Row and refuse to look at the hideous motors you may see pass by a ghostly carriage and a pair of high-steppers and the funny old lady just discernible from under her sunshade.

"Denys looked at this strange old lady in wonder.

'I don't know how you knew,' he said, 'but it is true. It is one of my dreams. I have many.'

'Don't marry some one who will have no sympathy with your dream. I know a man who had just such a dream as yours. He has moved mountains to realise it. Now that he might do it he has a fashionable English wife and half a dozen scornful children who smile at his dreams of repossessing a ruined castle in Kerry, because it happened to be the cradle of his race.'

The crowd moved, broke up, and some one found Lady Caroline in her corner, a tall, distinguished-looking man, with a blue ribbon and a star on his breast.

'I have been looking everywhere for you, Lady Caroline,' he said. 'I am to have the great honour and pleasure of taking you in to supper.'

'And I am extremely hungry for it,' she

answered, addressing him by a name that made Denys stare reverently, ' and for your always delightful conversation.' ''

It is impossible not to be pleased when the novelist's art takes us along in this manner. There is the air of distinction about it all, the inevitable melancholy that a great lady is nearing the end of her long journey, there is the naive suggestion of an exquisite supper not very far out of our reach.

Mrs. Tynan brings out very clearly that the chief fault of Denys is really quite a good fault. He is full of impetuosity, he takes matters into his own hands and very nearly annoys his employer. All the way through we are quite conscious that Mrs. Tynan is dealing with a reaction. From being a great dreamer Denys becomes a great man of action. The transition carries with it a certain hardness and want of heart in the character of Denys. He jumps to conclusions and does not consider the preliminary steps. Mrs. Tynan without, as I say, concentrating on a psychological study to the exclusion of a story, allows Denys to develop himself quite logically.

If we are grateful to Mrs. Tynan for nothing else we can at least thank her for the descriptions she gives us of London in the days before the motors began to do their best to destroy the picturesqueness of the great city. Here is an exquisite glimpse of Oxford Street, in those far-off days when the jingling of the bells on the harness of the hansom horses made music, as they swept east and west and the old horse " 'buses " lumbered along. But that has all gone for ever and in its place we have the odious motor omnibuses and the only music the incessant hooting of the motor horns. We are only just beginning to realise that the streets have been robbed of much of their beauty by the passing of the horse-drawn hansoms and the horse-drawn " 'buses."

" Going down Oxford Street very slowly, for the street, still bathed in the westward-sinking sun, was thronged with vehicles ; although the shops were shut and the foot passengers wore a homeward-going, absorbed air, Denys was aware that many of the hansoms that passed him contained a pair of lovers. He was aware of the clasped hands, the eyes directed upon each other, the glowing and happy faces that sometimes, for decorum's sake, tried to conceal the state of things."

And there is the romantic touch about it all—
for what better setting for two handsome lovers
than a hansom ?

" Other couples again were lovers unashamed.
The hansom went smoothly for a few yards :
then jerked abruptly, held up by the hansom in
front. A bother, these frequent blocks ! The
lovers did not seem to mind. There was a
charmingly pretty girl with a piquant, irregular
face and a wide mouth, who said to the infatuated
man sitting beside her, and the words reached
Denys' ear : ' I do love this slow procession
down Oxford Street, don't you ? ' "

Of course, every lover would. And the London
traffic is very good to lovers, for it much prefers
them to the hurrying crowds all impatient lest one
second for money grubbing be lost.

Mrs. Tynan is always a thoroughly sympathetic
writer. She is broad-minded without acquiescing
in every kind of conduct. Quite gently now and
then she disagrees with her characters.

Like all novelists who can write a really good
story, by which I mean a story that has both
imagination and invention, Mrs. Tynan has considerable powers of description. Perhaps her type

of description can best be called " straightforward " description. I think that sometimes it is not quite realised how varied are the kinds of description. There is the very full kind of description which quite certainly characterises Sir Walter Scott. There is the elaborate description which was so natural to Oscar Wilde. Then there is the living description which is so excellently exemplified in Hardy's portrait of Egdon Heath. Again there is the almost violent description that comes out now and again in the writings of Charles Dickens. But Mrs. Tynan employs the simple and straightforward method of describing. She uses an economy of words, but is never mean. When the Arsenal is struck during a thunderstorm we have an example of this simple method of describing.

"That night's storm was long remembered. It was what the old people called a dry storm. All night long the earth and skies ached for the relief of rain which the torn and shattered heaven seemed powerless to release to them."

It would have been so easy to have turned this into a less simple kind of description, with a describing of the flashes, the country lit up by them, the feel of the atmosphere, when all we want to know is that there is a big thunderstorm and a good deal of noise with it !

Mrs. Tynan ends her story on a perfectly orthodox note. Denys gets the girl he wants and all is quite happy. It may be argued that such an ending is commonplace, trite and even cowardly. At the same time a novel that ends happily leaves a pleasant taste in the mouth, and the " ends " of many of our " very clever " works of fiction leave a taste the reverse of pleasant.

*   *   *   *   *

If we turn to a popular novel of Mrs. Tynan's, " A Fine Gentleman," we discover that she is equally skilful in dealing with a young man of a completely different type from Denys. Mrs. Tynan is not in any way-class conscious in that she is awkward with any particular class of person. In the novel I am considering now we have to deal with a young officer. No kind of individual offers less scope to the novelist. As a rule young officers are quite well-mannered, fond of dancing and hunting, and are not in any way outstanding. Without being unmoral they do not usually stand out against the accepted code, which

I am bound to say is not particularly stringent. And yet without in any way encroaching on the bounds of probability Mrs. Katherine Tynan manages to give us a story about an officer who is neither a prig nor a prude and will not budge one inch from the high standard he has set himself. Such is the main background of this charming story.

The chief charm of Michael Drummond is the fact that he is quite unaware of his charm. He does not notice (as he would if he happened to be a novelist !) that eyes have a habit of looking in his direction. He is without embarrassment because he is unconscious of the speculation and interest that he arouses. He is even unaware of this on a P. and O. liner ! So we see Michael on a liner dropping down from Tilbury, not noticing that he is being noticed by the type of woman that is bred on all liners—the type of woman who means to throw convention overboard at the first available opportunity.

" A good many bright eyes had looked his way. His bronzed face, in striking contrast with his blue eyes, his voice, his smile, his politeness, his thoughtfulness for others had attracted much love and liking. He was unconscious of it, unconscious of his difference from the bored indifferent young men who hung about the ballrooms."

No—young Michael Drummond is that very rare specimen, an unspoilt young man. Mrs. Tynan shows him to us as a precious flower, something white and almost spotless. His life leads him through difficult places, but his soul is ever in the ascendant and no blows can smash him or alter the straightness of his life. Again Mrs. Tynan tells us, as though to emphasise the fact, that Michael is quite unaware of his fascination.

" He went back to India carrying with him, in one way or another, the images of three women. It made him less susceptible, less aware of the beauty of women than he had been on the home-ward voyage. Many bright eyes looked his way without his being aware of it, though he never failed in his social duties and was always ready to dance or do anything else required of him."

In other words—he is naturally a " good " fellow and he is also a GOOD fellow. That is the impression we derive from Mrs. Tynan's story. Michael sees straight because his heart is pure, he is pure because he sees straight. He causes of course a certain amount of disappointment on the liner, especially as he writes so many letters. And to whom do young officers write letters except to young ladies?

" ' He has got engaged during his leave—they all do,' a young lady said petulantly to Mrs. Weldon, whose husband belonged to Michael Drummond's regiment."

Michael Drummond is one of those delightful people who is called upon to carry out any task that no one else cares to have to undertake. If there is any bad news to be broken it is he who is made to break it. When, then, Vanston gets scooped by a married vampire just as his fiancee is coming out to marry him, dear Michael is given the horrid task of meeting the lady at Bombay and telling her that she has unfortunately been superseded. Well indeed does Mrs. Tynan give us the dialogue between Vanston and Drummond. There is all the halting misery of the wretched little faithless ass who is dragged about by a married woman like a puppy dog on a string. There is Drummond's unspoken contempt for this brother officer who is beaten by one of life's most deadly complications. There is no military station in India or elsewhere which is free from the loathsome type of married woman who will ruin any young officer so long as there are young officers foolish enough to be ruined. The worst of Vanston is that he is a fool. Anything but this could be forgiven him.

"The poor damned young fool! Michael Drummond was not given to violence. His violences were kept for special occasions. Perhaps this was one of them. He could not keep the expletive out of his thoughts."

This is important in understanding Drummond. He is so careful not to say anything hurtful if possible. He will not say a damn—he will think one!

"'Don't talk nonsense, Vanston,' he said roughly. 'You've got to live and make up for being a fool. If you won't face this lady what is to be done? Have you anything to suggest?'

The boy looked up at him.

'I thought—would you meet Vera? Make it as easy for her as possible? You would do it better than anyone else. . . .'

His eyes were fixed on Michael Drummond.

They seemed to have dropped back into the deep sockets. The young face had become incredibly haggard.

Pity sharp as a sword.

' Upon my word you are damned cool, youngster,' Michael Drummond said, but there was no anger in his voice. He heard himself as though he listened to some one else speaking :

' If I am to do this thing for you,' he said, ' you might as well tell me her name.' "

The dialogue here runs easily and naturally. It is pleasant to read and has that suggestion of coming excitement which is so necessary to the novelist who relies on getting over a good story. Mrs· Tynan has a great power of never holding up the tale. Not very long ago Mr. Chesterton in an essay somewhere (I haven't the least idea where) remarked that a certain author took you to an inn in one of his novels, went into a discussion of the mental state of the chief character for many pages and then remembered that everyone was still in the inn. That is a very pronounced characteristic of much modern fiction. This extraordinary fashion of dalliance, this remarkable habit of holding up the story for a kind of psychological digression, almost a kind of investigation, not by a novelist but by a brain specialist. Now Mrs. Tynan does not do this. She gets along through her story quickly and yet without any suggestion of rushing. It all seems when we read " A Fine Gentleman " quite natural that Drummond should not only meet the lady at Bombay, but fall in love with her and marry her. And then, alas! it seems just as natural that she should die and leave poor Michael all alone by himself. The whole affair is sad and even tragic. Mrs. Tynan sums it up briefly.

" How the marriage might or might not have turned out, was decided within the year. The Regiment was back at Aldershot when Nancy Weldon heard the end of it. She had gone off to be with Michael. Vera's baby had just fluttered into life and out of it and Vera had followed after a few hours."

Such a silly little tragedy that does not in the least affect the great world. But it is these little tragedies which are the very backbone of the novelist's art. Where would he be without them ?

I have already referred to Mrs. Tynan's fine and yet simple power of description. There is a charming picture of the Madeleine and what that great church and the Catholic Faith can do to smash all that sensual side of the French which makes them so misunderstood and in some ways misjudged. Michael is in Paris and he is struck, as everyone surely must be, by the strange and startling complexity of the French people.

" The great church had been cool and dim after the street. There were not many sight-seers ; it was early. There was Mass going on at a side altar and there were men standing, middle-aged and old, waiting for the Holy Communion. Stiff as ramrods, some of them, their proud heads bent in prayer. Old soldiers, obviously aristocrats. There was something about them that had taken his imagination. A strange people, the French. He remembered the things he had seen on the bookstalls, in the shops, the cinemas, the theatres, in the hands of girls and boys, reading shamelessly in a public conveyance. By such as these old men should France be saved."

Indeed these men shall save France, for here is the other side, the sensuality, the lust for sex, the side of Paris which no more represents France than Soho represents London.

" All that press of human beings and the screaming of the jazz band. There were black men dancing with white girls."

Over and over again is it thus brought out how admirable a descriptionist is Mrs. Katherine Tynan. London with the jingling of the hansoms— a liner with its romance—Paris with its Mass at the one end and a low dance hall at the other. One more little peep at Paris, and this time when her lovely and delicate streets warm with the summer sun, greet us with gestures of welcome and love.

" They drove to the Gare du Nord through the sunlit streets filled with people. The summer night had got into the heads of the Parisians. All those houses must have given up their inhabitants to the street pavements. Here and there where was an open place there was a fair and there were booths and a blaring band and the people were dancing. There was a smell of roses and syringa in the air. Paris would not sleep till morning."

London may try as much as she likes, she will

not get this atmosphere. And your sturdy English-
man does not want it. It would try his imagination
too much.

*   *   *   *   *

In " The Face in the Picture " Mrs. Tynan relies
on one of the simplest of themes. Dick Trevelyan
goes to stay at the country house of an old school-
fellow and there falls in love so much with the face
of a girl in a picture, that he determines he must
find her in the flesh. The subsequent story deals
with his curious adventures while he pursues his
search. Mrs. Tynan leads us into some strange
adventures, but they are never forced or unnatural.
In this kind of story she is not in any sense whatever
a pioneer. She does not wish to try the novel in a
new form, but is content to rely on an old kind of
" stock " tale. And it is both courageous and sensible to do so. We have evolved from the type of
tales that Mrs. Tynan writes, but I am inclined to
think that we shall revolve back to them. We are
quite often in grave danger of having thrust upon
us a kind of fiction which is nothing more or less
than pen portraits of neurotic or erotic people.
Catholic novelists have a very great chance in keeping

this kind of hothouse fiction in the background. Novelists like Mrs. Tynan do no little to help. It can be said all the way through that her work invariably infers Catholicism. It is naturally not there in quite the same way of presentment as that presented by either Father Benson or John Ayscough. But it is not necessary to read between the lines to know that Mrs. Tynan stands rigidly for all that Catholics hold dear. She shows us that clean, healthy fiction, not by any means great fiction, can still hold and interest us. She proves to us (and it needs proving in this century) that love is a clean and glorious romance, and not something fleshly and sensual.

* * * * *

The Catholic Novelists of whom I have endeavoured to give some picture in this book are indeed entrusted with the guardianship of fiction. I do not think it will be suggested by anyone that they have failed in this guardianship. A large and growing fiction which stands, if not actually hostile, at least aloof, from what they hold as Catholics, needs to be leavened more and more. Catholic Novelists in this age are in the minority in numbers. In the matter of talent they include some of our finest creators of fiction. I have considered seven out of those Catholic Novelists who appear to me to be outstanding. But the breath of the Catholic Faith sweeps down and permeates all their writings.

The Catholic Novelists dwell alone, and on all sides the busy world rushes heedlessly by. It may read what these Novelists who are Catholics write. But it seldom if ever pauses and considers what they really do stand for. For they stand all together for a Church and Faith which in a daily changing world do not change. They stand for a philosophy which has the Keys not only of Earth but of Heaven and Hell also.

Whether expressed or merely implied, these seven Catholic Novelists stand for the things that really matter. The day will come when those who have been entrusted with the gift of writing will be called to give an account of their use of this priceless gift. These Catholic Novelists have used their great gifts in the work of keeping fiction pure and lovely. For this they may well hear, when their call comes (to two it has come already), the Divine eulogy which, being interpreted, reads that those who are good and faithful servants will enter to their reward.

In this life these Novelists have gained great

awards for their work. But of all their awards, that which will be to them of the greatest value will be the knowledge that as Catholic Novelists they have through their books helped to spread the Faith, that Faith which endures even unto the end of the world.

THE END

SOME PRESS OPINIONS OF PATRICK
BRAYBROOKE'S WORKS

" While he is no servile flatterer of the successful his shafts do not wound."—*The Times Literary Supplement*.

" Mr. Braybrooke has the merit of letting cheerfulness frequently break in."—EDMUND BLUNDEN in *The Nation*.

" Sententious—never pretentious."—GERALD GOULD in *The Daily News*.

" Brilliant."—*The Bookman*.

" Readers who do not agree with all of Mr. Braybrooke's conclusions may admire the vigour with which they are expressed."—*The Daily Herald*.

" Acute critic that he is."—*Public Opinion*.

" Touches on all the important points."—*The Saturday Review*.

" Mr. Braybrooke is evidently one of those rare and pleasant people who are determined to find something to praise in any successful writer. Modern criticism could well do with more of his generous attitude towards Literary Creation."—*The Catholic Times*.

" Mr. Braybrooke is the perfect critic."—*Edinburgh Evening News*.

" Congratulations to Mr. Braybrooke on a very capable piece of Literary Criticism."—MRS. G. K. CHESTERTON in *G. K.'s Weekly*.

" A fine tribute."—*The Universe*.

" A novel marked by true sympathy and understanding."—SIR WILLIAM DAVIES in *The Western Mail*.

" We can say of the author as he says of Max Beerbohm, ' His charming essays are the reflection of a subtle and an observing mind.' "—*Boston Evening Transcript*.

" He adopts the best and simplest method of criticism."—*New York Times*.

" One of the interesting writers of to-day."—*Army and Navy Gazette*.

" He has done some notable work in literary criticism."—*The Methodist Recorder*.

" Has a high reputation as a literary critic."—*Church of England Newspaper*.

" The author has already thoroughly established himself as a reliable literary analyst and guide."—*The Librarian*.

" One of the sanest of modern critics."—CHARLES WELLS in *The Bristol Mirror*.

" He is really too good a writer for his talent to be wasted."—*The Times of India*.

" Mr. Braybrooke's pleasant task is to write kind things about living authors."—*The Daily Telegraph*.

" We welcome such frankly individual work."—*Birmingham Post*.

" He writes easily and fluently."—*South Wales News*.

" Has a big reputation on both sides of the Atlantic."—*Dublin Evening Herald*.

" Must be congratulated once more on a masterpiece."—*Current Literature*.

Printed at
The Mayflower Press, Plymouth.   William Brendon & Son, Ltd.